MARRAKECH

in your pocket

D1323749

MAIN CONTRIBUTOR: MELISSA SHALES

PHOTOGRAPH CREDITS
All photos supplied by The Travel Library:
The Travel Library A Birkett 21 (l), 54; Stuart Black 42(t), 71(b), 73, 77; Lee Frost front cover, back cover, 4-5, 9, 11, 23, 27, 29, 30, 36, 38, 39, 42(b), 45, 46, 47, 50, 52, 53, 56, 57, 59, 75, 85, 89, 90, 91, 92, 95, 97, 99, 101, 103, 115, 117, 121; John R Jones 17, 25, 32, 55, 82, 109, 125; Hassam Nadim title page, 8, 13, 19, 49, 79; Christine Osborne 21(r), 37, 62(b), 63, 67, 68, 69; Grant Pritchard 43(r), 81; R Richardson 48.
ffotograff Patricia Aithie 7, 111; Mary Andrews 64, 84; Bob Pearson 60, 66.
Greg Balfour Evans 40-41, 43(l), 71(t), 74, 106; Alexandra Taibel 44.
Sylvia Cordaiy Photo Library Les Gibbon 62(t); Renee Jasper 35: Nick Rains 72; Roy Westlake 105.

Front cover: Jemaa el Fna, Marrakech
back cover: the apothecaries' souk, Marrakech
title page: Berber girl and child

While every effort is made to ensure that the information in this guide is as accurate and up-to-date as possible, detailed information is constantly changing. The publisher cannot accept responsibility for any consequences resulting from changes in information, errors or omissions.

MANUFACTURE FRANÇAISE DES PNEUMATIQUES MICHELIN

Place des Carmes-Déchaux – 63000 Clermont-Ferrand (France)

© Michelin et Cie. Propriétaires-Éditeurs 2002

Dépôt légal Jan 02 – ISBN 2-06-100165-3 – ISSN 1272-1689

No part of this publication may be reproduced in any form

without the prior permission of the publisher.

Printed in Spain 01/02

MICHELIN TRAVEL PUBLICATIONS
Hannay House
39 Clarendon Road
WATFORD Herts WD17 1JA - UK
☎ (01923) 205240
www.ViaMichelin.com

MICHELIN TRAVEL PUBLICATIONS
Michelin North America
One Parkway South
GREENVILLE, SC 29615
☎ 1-800 423-0485
www.ViaMichelin.com

CONTENTS

INTRODUCTION

Built as a garrison town and trading post at the
point where mountains and plains meet the
desert, on the border between civilisation and
lawlessness, Marrakech still has two faces – one
looking towards the east, with all the exotic
splendour of Arabia, the other firmly facing
north to the comforts and luxuries of France.
Life in the medina is conducted behind high,
featureless walls, while the inner courtyards are
a riot of mosaic, stucco carving and gardens.
The side streets are quiet in daytime but
thronging with shoppers and children once the
sun goes down. The summer sun has taught
the Marrakchi to live inside out.

   In many ways this little coral-red city is the
ideal short-break destination, with just enough
sightseeing to keep you entertained but not so
much that you have to work at it. It has winter
sunshine aplenty, wonderful food and hotels,
excellent shopping, and endlessly fascinating
street life. Within a couple of hours' drive are

*Late afternoon and
the food stalls and
street entertainers
begin to set up on
Place Jemaa el Fna,
while spectators
gather on the café
balconies.*

spectacular mountains and miles of golden sand beach. The people are charming, the food delicious, and it is less than three hours by air from most European cities. It is little wonder that Marrakech is rapidly becoming one of the trendiest destinations in the world.

Yet for all the many tourists, it is still firmly attached to its roots. The souks may have many souvenir stalls but they also sell everything from great piles of mint, brought down from the mountains by donkey, to plastic buckets and net curtains. A luridly grinning sign marks the local dentist, while round the corner a queue of people waits for a trim at the outdoor barbers. In the magical Jemaa el Fna, filled with firewalkers and food stalls, most of the crowds which gather each evening are composed of locals, as eager as the tourists for entertainment. Sit on a café balcony overlooking the square, with a glass of fresh pressed orange juice, and watch dancers, acrobats and swirling throngs, and soak up the magic that pervades the air.

GEOGRAPHY

Tucked into the northwest corner of Africa, facing Spain across the narrow Straits of Gibraltar, Morocco is both an ancient and modern country – a proud historic empire, whose modern borders were actually put in place only in 1975. It covers a total of 710 850 sq km, with 2 900km (1 812 miles) of Atlantic coast and 500km (300 miles) of Mediterranean coast.

The landscape is immensely varied, from the Saharan sand dunes of the deep south to a fertile coastal plain and the high snow-capped peaks of the Atlas mountains, three ranges which run parallel across the country, from southwest to northeast – the Moyen Atlas (Middle Atlas) in the north, the Haut Atlas (High Atlas) in the middle and the Anti Atlas to the south. The highest point in the country is Jbel Toubkal (4 167m/13 670ft), in the High Atlas, just south of Marrakech.

Between the ranges are well-watered, fertile valleys, which create a lush garden in much of this immensely scenic country. Marrakech sits in one of these broad valleys, about 170km (106 miles) from the coast, surrounded by huge groves of date palms, olive and citrus trees.

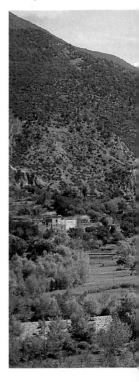

High mountains and deep, fertile valleys sprinkled with Berber villages are just a short drive from Marrakech.

Economy

The economy is relatively stable, with both inflation and economic growth running at 2-3 percent a year. However, it is balanced on a precarious knife edge, with huge amounts of foreign debt, a rapidly growing population and small taxable class. Marrakech is Morocco's premier tourist destination and is also the second largest commercial centre in the country (after

Casablanca). Tourism, crafts and trade are the big money-spinners but other local industries include flour-mills, milk processing plants, breweries, canning factories, cement production plants and, increasingly, textiles. There has also been a concerted effort to maintain and revive traditional crafts, with 81 craft cooperatives in the Marrakech region alone. Agriculture (fruit, wheat and barley) is the main employer but tourism, fishing and phosphates are important to the economy.

Threshing wheat the traditional way, in the Dadès region of the High Atlas mountains.

HISTORY

The city of Marrakech was founded in 1061 but people have lived and traded in the area almost continuously for at least 50 000 years. The Berbers, thought to be the aboriginal inhabitants of the region, were certainly in the area by the time the Phoenicians began trading along the coast as far south as Essaouira around 1200 BC, and proved a military thorn in the side of the Romans throughout their rule of the region (from the fall of Carthage in 146 BC to the arrival of the Vandals in AD 429).

The Arab Invasions

In 684 the first wave of Islamic Arabs swept west, under the command of **Oqba ben Nafi** of the **Umayed dynasty** in Damascus, naming the region *Maghreb el Aksa* ('land farthest west'). As the Arabs took the valleys and the plains, the Berbers retreated to the mountains but they were pragmatic people who recognised the benefits of power and liked the message of Islam. Most converted and joined the cause. By the time **Moussa ibn Nasr** led the invasion of Spain in 711, his commander, Tarik ben Ziad, and much of his army was Berber.

The first person really to unite Morocco was **Idriss ben Abdallah (Idriss I)**, a descendant of the Prophet Mohammed, who arrived in 788, fleeing after a failed revolt against the Caliph of Baghdad. Impressed by his piety, the Berbers appointed him their spiritual and political leader and he founded the first Arab dynasty in Morocco. He was killed in 791 but his son, **Idriss II**, born after his father's death, went on to found Fès. The **Idrissid dynasty** did not survive his death in 828, when the country was split into a series of small kingdoms under the rule of his nine sons and the power of the state became diluted and vulnerable to attack.

The Almoravids (1062-1147)

The fiercely Islamic *El Murabetun* (later corrupted to Almoravids) were desert-dwelling nomads from modern Mauritania. They began their violent expansion deep in the Sahara in the 10C. In 1060, under the leadership of the fanatically pious **Youssef ben Tachfine**, they turned north, setting up a garrison camp in a broad, fertile valley just north of the High Atlas mountains. It was to become their capital city, Marrakech. To cope with the shortage of water and irrigate the thousands of date palms essential to their survival, they built a complex system of wells and underground channels (*khettara*) to funnel water down from the

Built by the 12C Sultan Ali ben Youssef, the Koubba Ba'Adiyn is the only remaining Almoravid building left in Marrakech. Its decorated dome and horseshoe arches are features echoed in later Moroccan architecture.

9

mountains; they are still used today to water the city gardens.

From here, Ben Tachfine pressed north, conquering Fès in 1069. Within a few short years he was in control of a vast empire, stretching from Niger in the south to Algeria in the east and much of Spain to the north.

The Almoravid era was never entirely peaceful but it was a time of prosperity. While Youssef moved north, his son, Ali, gradually transformed the city from a nomadic camp into a permanent settlement built with the local red mud. Using skilled builders from Andalucia, he embellished the city with palaces and gardens, mosques and souks, all surrounded by high protective walls. Marrakech became a centre of learning and the arts.

It was the good life that eventually proved to be the downfall of the Almoravids, as the physical and religious discipline of the Berbers was undermined by the softer and decidedly sybaritic delights of the Andalucian courts.

The Almohads (1147-1269)

In 1130 another puritanical leader arrived to challenge them. His name was **Mohammed ibn Toumert**, leader of the Mouwahhidine (Unitarian) sect, who lived at Tinmel in the High Atlas mountains. In 1147 his heir, **Abd el-Moumen**, the son of a potter, eventually conquered Marrakech, killing the last remaining Almoravids and demolishing any traces of their decadent lifestyle.

The Almohad dynasty lasted until 1269 and Marrakech flourished under its stewardship. One man in particular stands out from the crowd – **Yacoub el Mansour** (the Conqueror) who reigned from 1184-1190. Although he moved his capital to Seville for a time, he was responsible for much of the layout of Marrakech as it exists today, building the great

The Bab Agnaou, built in 1185 by Yacoub el Mansour as the entrance to the kasbah, was the only stone building in the city at the time, apart from the Koutoubia.

rampart walls, creating the Menara Gardens and erecting the imposing minaret of the Koutoubia Mosque. The city again became fashionable, and a world centre of spiritual and artistic study.

Inevitably, however, the Almohads also began to decline, their fortunes suffering after a massive defeat by Christian Spain in 1212, leaving them powerless to stop the advance of the ambitious Merenids.

The Merenids and Wattasids (1269-1524)

The Beni Merin, a nomadic tribe from the Algerian border region, were motivated more by greed than religion. They found it easy to take Fès and declare independence in 1213.

In 1230 the Sultan held onto Marrakech only with the aid of an army of 12 000 Christian soldiers lent to him by King Ferdinand of Castile and Leon. In 1269 the Merenids eventually took Marrakech and officially ended the Almohad dynasty.

They returned the capital to Fès, from where they ruled for nearly 250 years, while Marrakech declined into relative obscurity and poverty. Theirs was a civilised court, filled with scientists and geographers, such as the great traveller, Ibn Batouta. They created the first civil service, set aside the *mellahs* (Jewish areas) for those fleeing Christian Spain to live in safety, and founded a series of *medersas* (lodgings for the religious schools) to encourage learning and clean living. The Christian fightback in Spain was, however, proving too much for them and their empire slowly but irrevocably shrank. By 1465 there was room for yet another power struggle and the throne was snatched by the hereditary Vizir, **El Wattas**.

By now the European age of expansion had begun. Spain and Portugal both turned greedy eyes towards Morocco. Portugal invaded Asilah, kidnapping 5 000 of the Wattasid family and their slaves, and forced the court to sign over large areas of the west coast, including Essaouira, as ransom.

The Saadians (1554-1668)

By 1524 Marrakech was in a terrible state, threatened by the Portuguese to the west, by the Ottomans to the east, and largely ignored by the Wattasids in Fès. The Saadians were an Arabic people, descendents of the Prophet Mohammed, who had settled in the Drâa Valley, south of Marrakech, in the 12C. With their own lands threatened, their leader, **Mohammed ech Cheikh**, declared *jihad* (holy war), a popular cause amongst the embittered and embattled Moroccans. In 1525 they took Marrakech. By 1541 they had retaken many of the Portuguese territories and within a few years had deposed the sultan and conquered Fès. It was the end of Berber rule in Morocco.

In 1578, at Ksar el Kbir, came the final confrontation, known in history as the **Battle of the Three Kings**. On one side was a force of 50 000 Muslims, led by Sultan Abd el Malik, on the other the Portuguese king, Sebastian, and the deposed Sultan Mohammed el Mutawakkil. Trapped between two rivers, Sebastian and Mohammed both drowned; Abd el Malik died of fever. The battle and the kingdom were won by El Malik's brother, **Ahmed el-Mansour**, nicknamed **el Dehbi** (the Victorious and Golden), who funded a rebuilding of the

Afraid of supernatural retribution, Moulay Ismaïl walled up the Saadian tombs rather than plunder them, preserving their magnificence for future generations to wonder at.

country from the ransoms paid by the Portuguese prisoners of war.

Ahmed looked south to the gold mines of Niger and brought in thousands of slaves from the Sudan. It was an extraordinary era, mirrored across the civilised world, with Elizabeth I on the throne of England, François I in France, Suleyman the Magnificent ruling the Ottoman empire, Charles V ruling the Holy Roman Empire and Catherine the Great on the Russian throne. Marrakech was adorned with a fabulous new palace, El Badii, and a sprinkling of hammams, libraries, mosques and other grand public buildings. Once again it became a focus for trade in sugar, cotton, silk, slaves, gold, ivory and ostrich feathers.

As ever, it did not last. Eventually, the kingdom was split into two, then three, and chaos descended. In a series of bitter civil wars, Marrakech was plundered and destroyed, leaving little to mark the passing of the Saadians, other than a collection of magnificent tombs in Marrakech, walled up and hidden from the world until the 20C.

The Alaouites (1659 –   )

By 1666 the people of Fès were so disillusioned that they invited **Moulay Rachid** to take over the throne. He was an Arab, also descended from the Prophet Mohammed, whose people had settled in the southern Tafilalet area three centuries earlier. He managed to restore order and rebuild some of troubled Marrakech but, while it technically remained a joint capital for many years and was a wealthy trading centre for much of the 18-19C, the real powerbase had moved to Meknès. Marrakech was out in the cold.

Moulay Ismaïl (1672-1727) was the greatest of the early Alaouite sultans, a man of strong ambition and ruthless cruelty, who rebuilt Morocco into a great power, able to deal with the Europeans on equal terms. He also created an Imperial Guard of black slaves who became the real powerbrokers in Morocco on his death. Thirty years later, another fine ruler, **Mohammed ben Abdallah**, finally managed to curtail their excesses and began to restore the kingdom. Amongst his many achievements was the building of Essaouira, inviting in English, French and Jewish traders.

By the 19C, however, Europe's imperial ambitions were once again threatening the kingdom. France landed in Algeria in 1830 and had control by 1846; in 1860 a Spanish invasion was halted only with the aid of the British. By 1873, when **Moulay Hassan** acceded to the throne, various European governments were openly interfering in the running of the State, suggesting helpful ways of reforming the administration and tax collection, all of which inevitably gave them greater influence.

In 1906, at the **Conference of Algeciras**, 30 nations gathered to formalise spheres of influence while guaranteeing Moroccan sovereignty. In practice, Tangier became an international free port, and France and Spain were allowed in to 'restore order'. In 1912 the **Treaty of Fès** relieved Sultan Moulay Hafid of power, the Spanish hived off a chunk of the country in the south, and Morocco officially became a French protectorate, under the control of the French Resident-General, Louis Lyautey.

Lyautey fell in love with the country and its people and proved to be a sympathetic ruler, carefully preserving monuments and ancient cities, while building new cities and districts alongside them. Among his many projects was the construction of Guéliz, the new city of Marrakech. The French also introduced modern education and legislation, built roads and railways.

By the 1920s, however, trouble was brewing in the south and as the French tried to play the Arabs off against the Berbers, all they succeeded in doing was to create a strong nationalist movement. In 1943 the Istiqlal (Freedom) Party was formed and sent a request for independence to the sultan and the French. Most of its leaders were promptly arrested.

The independently-minded Sultan **Mohammed V** began to sympathise with the nationalists. Alarmed for the future of their personal wealth and privilege, a group of Moroccan nobles, under the leadership of the pasha of Marrakech, **Thami el Glaoui**, demanded that the sultan be deposed. In 1953 the sultan and his family were exiled to Madagascar and a puppet was placed on the throne. Violent protest followed and two years later El Glaoui had to admit defeat and ask for the sultan to be brought back.

Independence

In December 1956 Mohammed V returned to the throne as king of a constitutional, democratic monarchy. Morocco simultaneously gained full independence from France and Spain, and Tangier was returned to the kingdom. The only outstanding area was the Western Sahara, formerly Spanish territory, which was claiming independence.

In 1975 **King Hassan II** led a **Green March** of 350 000 unarmed Moroccans into the region, to reassert Morocco's sovereignty. After a few years of confusion – during which time a referendum under the aegis of the United Nations was considered – the new king, Mohammed VI, who had come to the throne on 23 July 1999, revived the peace process by considering granting a degree of autonomy to the region.

PEOPLE AND CULTURE

The aboriginal inhabitants of northwest Africa were christened *Barbari* (barbarians) by the Romans, a name corrupted over time to Berber. The proud, independent Berbers themselves prefer the name *Imazighen* ('free men'). In fact, the Berbers are made up of several different tribal peoples, speaking three different but related languages. Those in the High Atlas, near Marrakech, generally speak Tachelhit (also called Chleuh).

The Arabs began arriving in the late 7C and 8C in the initial wave of Islamic conquest that swept across North Africa. Over the centuries, the Berbers and Arabs have intermarried and few can now claim 'pure' blood. There is virtually no physical difference, although some mountain Berbers in remote areas have significantly paler skins and blue or green eyes. Around 60 percent of the population (including urban Berbers) speak Moroccan Arabic as their first language – a situation 'aided' by all schooling being conducted in that language and a distinct bias against rural education.

A traditional Berber encampment in the High Atlas.

Lifestyle tends to be affected more by whether you live in town or the countryside than by any ethnic history. Traditionally, the valleys and plains were known as the *bled el Makhzen* (the lands of government), while the mountains were referred to as the *bled es Siba* (the lawless lands).

Other ethnic groups in the country include the Haratins, a small group of black Africans or Arab-black mixed race people descended mainly from Sudanese slaves imported in the 17C, although some are undoubtedly descended from West African traders; the Sahrawi, native to the Western Sahara; and Europeans, mainly French and Spanish, who make up around 5 percent of the population.

The Statistics

Morocco currently has a population of around 30.1 million, of whom over 50 percent are under 25. Over 55 percent live in the cities. Average life expectancy is 69 years for men, 71 for women. 'Greater' Marrakech now has a population of just under 1 million, of whom around 184 000 live in the medina.

The country is split dramatically between the haves and have-nots, with around 13 percent living below the poverty line and a sharp divide between rural and urban lifestyles. In spite of recent improvements, some 52 percent of people are still illiterate (rising to 82.3 percent amongst rural women). Urban women have an average of 2.2 children each; in the rural areas they have 3.5. In the cities 89 percent have clean drinking water, 84 percent have electricity, 70 percent have a fridge and 91 percent have a TV. In rural areas only 11 percent have clean drinking water, 12 percent have electricity, 8 percent have a fridge but 45 percent have access to TV!

Religion

Islam is the official state religion, followed to a greater or lesser degree by most Moroccans, but there is little sign of fundamentalist activity, and freedom of worship is guaranteed by the constitution.

Muslims believe in one God, Allah, following a lifestyle laid down in the *Koran* by his 7C Prophet Mohammed. There are five duties or 'pillars of Islam' – prayer, five times a day, announced by the muezzin from the minarets; the simple creed 'There is no God but Allah and Mohammed is his Prophet'; the giving of alms to the poor; fasting during the holy month of Ramadan; and the pilgrimage to Mecca.

Morocco traditionally also had a significant Jewish population, most of whom have now emigrated to Israel. There are only around 10-15 000 remaining, mainly in the historic cities. In remote rural areas there is a sprinkling of Berber Christians, whose forebears either escaped conversion to Islam in the 8C or were reconverted by the Portuguese during their brief occupation.

These young boys from El-Kelaâ M'Gouna, in the Dadès Valley, are attending a Koranic school, where they are taught Islamic beliefs and to read the Koran.

The Monarchy

For centuries, Morocco was an absolute monarchy but, after independence in 1956, the sultan took the title of king and the country became a democratic constitutional monarchy. There is a parliament (with an indirectly elected Chamber of Counsellors and a directly elected Chamber of Representatives) and a prime minister. Even so, the majority of power remains in the hands of the king, a figure treated with awe, not only as head of State but as a direct descendant of the Prophet. Traditionally, the king is always married but his wife has no public role.

The present king, Mohammed VI, came to the throne in 1999, at the age of 36. A highly educated and sophisticated man, he is popular with his people and is working hard to improve their lot, with an increased emphasis on education and women's rights among other social issues.

Moroccan Women

The Constitution gives Moroccan women equal rights under law. Traditionally, however, they have remained housebound and uneducated – even the shopping is still done by the men in many rural communities. Women may own property but their husband is expected to have control of it and, while some 25 percent of the workforce is female, few women ever obtain real power. There is an increasingly powerful feminist lobby, however, and a new national council, Moudawana, has been set up to revise Moroccan family law in line with United Nations guidelines. Meanwhile, religious traditionalists are fighting a strong rearguard action and it will be a long time before rural women, at least, see any real change in their situation.

Moroccan Dress

Moroccan dress is ideally suited to the climate and often far more comfortable than western dress; even the most sophisticated and westernised Marrakchi will revert to traditional garments during their time off.

Basic garments for both men and women include the *gandoura* (a collarless cotton smock); the *kaftan*, a full-length light cotton robe with an embroidered neck, for wearing inside the house; and the *djellaba*, a hooded robe, often made of wool, for outdoor wear. On their feet they wear *babouches* (soft, flat, backless leather slippers). In the cold weather they wrap themselves in a *burnous* (an all-encompassing woollen cloak, with a pointed hood).

Few women now wear the all-concealing black *haik*, though significant numbers still wear a headscarf and *litham* (a small veil covering the lower half of the face).

MUST SEE

Place Jemaa el Fna★★

The main square at the heart of the medina, **Place Jemaa el Fna★★**, looks like a carpark in the early morning but, as the day progresses, so the crowds gather, drawn in by story-tellers, snake-charmers and other assorted buskers. By the **evening★★★** the place is thick with food stalls and crowds, an ever-changing, fascinating parade of entertainment.

The Souks★★

It can take days to explore the vast market which has been the geographical and emotional heart of Marrakech since the city was first founded. With its outer fringes dedicated to souvenirs, this is a fascinating place to wander, with everything from herbalists to food stalls, iron-workers to jewellers, bakers and leather-workers, their tiny shops ringing to the sound of hammers and tills. Take a guide or expect to get lost in the maze.

Koutoubia★★★

One of the earliest, largest and architecturally finest mosques in Morocco, the **Koutoubia★★★** was built by Yacoub el Mansour in the 12C. Non-Muslims are not allowed inside but you can admire the exterior, in particular the magnificent minaret, still the tallest building in the city.

Tombeaux Saâdiens★★★
(Saadian Tombs)

The tombs of the late-16C Saadian dynasty were walled up and accessible only via the mosque, so saved from later pillaging. The French created a narrow access passage, opening these wonderfully flamboyant monuments to tourism.

Jardin Majorelle★★
(Majorelle Garden)

The French artist, Jacques Majorelle, who lived here from 1922 to 1962, used a bold mix of planting, water and colour to create these wonderfully sculptural gardens, which are at once peaceful and inspirational. The garden is now owned by Yves Saint-Laurent.

Palais de la Bahia★★
(Bahia Palace)

This sumptuous riad, with its gardens planted with orange trees and cypress, patios surrounded with *zellij*-decorated rooms and wood painted ceilings, has all the magnificence of an Arab palace.

Âït-Benhaddou★★

It is little wonder that this desert kasbah is one of Morocco's most visited villages and has been used as a set for many films. Its jumbled maze of deep red decorated walls and crenellated towers blend into the barren and arid landscape from which it was created.

Essaouira★★

Essaouira is an enchanting coastal resort to explore, with its characteristic whitewashed buildings with their blue shutters and doors, the colourful harbour, the **Skala ramparts★** and bustling **souks★**.

Vallée du Drâa★★★

The contrast of this sumptuous, fertile valley, liberally punctuated with palm oases and *ksour*, winding its way through bare and rugged mountains, is a powerful and spectacular sight.

Vallée du Dadès★★

Nestling below the purple summits of the Atlas, the massive silhouettes of superb kasbahs with their defensive towers rise up from a desolate landscape punctuated only by green oases.

Sacks of herbs and dried potions in the apothecaries' souk, Marrakech.

Finding Your Feet

When General Lyautey became governor of
Morocco, he carefully sited the new developments
away from the old walled cities – a decision that
probably had as much to do with health, security
and comfort as his well-documented sensitivity to
the local culture and architecture. At the time,
Marrakech was in a parlous state of poverty and
decay.

Whatever the motive, the happy result was
Marrakech's split personality. One half of the city is
the ancient medina, a rabbit warren of narrow dark
alleys encircled by high medieval walls, the other a
planned new town of broad boulevards and plazas.
Both, however, are largely built of the local red
earth and all subsequent builders have followed the
old diktat that no building should ever rise higher
than the minaret of the Koutoubia. The result is a
charming low-rise city that glows red-gold at sunset
against an achingly beautiful background of snow-
capped mountains. Sadly but inevitably, it is now
being surrounded by an urban sprawl of ugly but
utilitarian apartment blocks and light industry.

It is easy to find your way in Guéliz, the new city
to the west, but the old city, the medina, is a totally
inexplicable maze. Distances are not great but you
may seem to be driving around in circles, to find a
way through the city walls or through streets wide
enough to take a car. Place Jemaa el Fna is roughly
at the centre. Immediately to its north are the
souks; the imperial sights are all to the south.

Most of the time the easiest way to get around is
on foot. If you get lost, someone will always help
you find your way but it is probably sensible to use a
guide at first (*see* p.124). Many of the smaller alleys
don't have names or are not marked. The best
method is to find your way by landmarks (a city
gate, mosque, school, hospital etc); pinpoint the
nearest and memorise the route from there. If in
doubt, pay a local child to help or phone and ask
someone to fetch you.

THE MEDINA★★★

Getting hopelessly lost in the back streets of the medina – and getting to know the neighbourhood children.

Gates punctuate the city walls which once protected the medina.

The **medina★★★** began life as a garrison camp in 1060, under the leadership of the Almoravid leader, Youssef ben Tachfine. Over the next 40 years, as these nomadic tent dwellers gradually converted to a stationary lifestyle, the city grew organically. The original walls probably followed roughly the same lines as those of today. Within them space was left for a great mosque (on the site of the Koutoubia), a parade ground and meeting place (Place Jemaa el Fna) and the souks, but the bulk of the housing within the walls grew up with no structured planning, creating the intricate web of alleys that survives until this day.

Little more than the ground plan survives of the Almoravid city; the earliest buildings surviving today are those of their successors, the 12C Almohads and the greatest

monuments belong to the 16-17C Saadian dynasty. Most domestic buildings are from the 18-19C. Since the fall of the Saadians in 1668, the city slowly but inexorably declined, the grand mansions of the medina began to rot and, with the arrival of the French, the business centre moved to Guéliz, along with many of the wealthier inhabitants.

Plenty of people still live in the medina but most are now poor and much of the housing is in a poor state of repair. The arrival of tourists is helping to reverse the trend. The Moroccans are generally happy to sell their tumble-down houses to Europeans, who possess the funds for restoration, and move to smart new suburban apartments. So far, everyone is happy. There is, however, a real danger that this process could suck the lifeblood from the medina and turn it into a historical theme park.

IMPERIAL MARRAKECH

The Koutoubia★★★

(*Av. Mohammed V, on the western edge of the medina, near Bab Djid*)

The **Koutoubia★★★** is the tallest building in Marrakech and also one of the finest mosques in North Africa. It received its name (Mosque of the Booksellers) from the cluster of bookshops that grew up at its feet during its life as a religious school. These days they have given way to a broad open plaza, which allows the thousands of tour groups to gaze up at the minaret with ease and awe. Next to it is the site of the original Almoravid kasbah, the **Dar el Hajar** (House of Stone).

When the Almohads arrived, they demolished the original Almoravid mosque and replaced it with their own but, in their haste, they built it out of true alignment to Mecca and had to take it down. An army of

Each face of the landmark Koutoubia minaret has a different decorative design.

pillar stumps marks its position.

The existing Koutoubia was completed in 1158, during the reign of Abd el-Moumen. It is a covered mosque (90m/295ft long and 60m/197ft wide), with plain white walls and 17 columns of pillars, linked by horseshoe arches, and five domes along the central nave. Non-Muslims are not allowed inside.

Instead, they marvel at the magnificent **minaret**, actually completed by Yacoub el Mansour and similar to his other grand projects, the Giralda in Seville and the Hassan Tower in Rabat. The square tower is 12m/39ft square at the base and nearly 77m (250ft) high. Inside it has a ramp, broad enough to ride a horse up, connecting six delicately ornamented rooms. Each of the asymmetric windows has a different design. At the top, a narrow band of blue tiles is all that remains of the original ceramic and stucco decoration; the domed lantern is topped by three gilded balls. According to one version of the legend, the originals were solid gold, said to have been made from the jewellery of the sultan's wife in penance for having eaten three grapes during the Ramadan fast.

To the Kasbah Gates

Across the road is the **Ensemble Artisanal** (*Av. Mohammed V*), an excellent place for shopping, a series of small State-sponsored craft workshops and galleries that serve as a training ground and offer good quality products at fair prices.

Cross back and walk through the gardens behind the Koutoubia, admiring the minaret from all angles. Across the road to the right is **La Mamounia** (*Av. Houmman el Fetouaki*), one of the great historic hotels of Africa, built by the French in 1923 as the railway hotel, just inside the city walls. Over the intervening years it has hosted the great, the good and the glamorous, from Winston Churchill to Elton John. The décor is an eclectic but definitely luxurious mix of art deco and traditional Moroccan; the whole place oozes money (not least the casino) but pride of place must go to the 20-acre gardens, the **Arset el Mamoun**. These were originally laid out in the 18C as a wedding present for Prince Moulay Mamoun, the son of Sultan Mohammed ben Abdallah. A drink on the terrace will entitle you to wander through a paradise of quiet green extravagance, perfumed by roses, oranges and jasmine.

Back along the main road, turn right into Place Youssef ben Tachfine. On the right, opposite the petrol station, is an insignificant crenellated building, the humble **tomb of Youssef ben Tachfine**, the founder of Marrakech. It is open to the sky, as no room is deemed big enough to hold this great warrior spirit, but sadly is not open to non-Muslims. If you peer through the window grille, you can just see the tomb.

Traditional opulence and exhuberant Moroccan decoration greet the rich and famous in the Mamounia.

From here, walk south along Rue Sidi Moumen (Sidi Mimoun). On the right is a massive building site, destined, at the time of writing, to become the new royal palace. A little further on are two gates at right angles. The one facing you (with roads running underneath) is the gate through the city walls, **Bab er Robb**. On your left is the delicately carved **Bab Agnaou★**, which translates colourfully as the Gate of the Hornless Ram – or more probably, Gate of the Blacks (i.e. leading to Black Africa). It was built in 1185 by Yacoub el Mansour as the entrance to the kasbah. It was the only stone building in the city at the time, apart from the Koutoubia, and is the only remaining Almohad gate (*see* p.11).

To its left is the **Mosquée d'El-Mansour** (El Mansour Mosque), built in 1190, also by Yacoub el Mansour. It has been restored frequently but the decoration on the minaret is original. A door on the far side is the original entrance to the Saadian Tombs; tourists must walk through the gate and small souk and turn right along Rue Kasbah to the ticket office.

The green-tiled revêtement and blue zellij decorations on the minaret of the El Mansour Mosque are unrestored.

Tombeaux Saâdiens*** (Saadian Tombs)

These magnificent tombs are the only ancient monuments in Marrakech to survive in pristine form, chiefly because they were walled up by Alaouite Sultan Moulay Ismaïl. It was the French who carefully tunnelled through the outer wall in 1917 to create the narrowest of access paths for non-Muslims. You are unlikely have the place to yourself but the frustration of the long queues is worthwhile, as you enter the small but enchanting cemetery garden, reserved, long before the arrival of the Saadians, for the descendants of the Prophet.

It was with the arrival of the Saadians in the 16C that the cemetery began to assume its current form. Altogether there are 66 members of the dynasty buried here, along with many favoured household retainers (in the mainly anonymous outdoor graves). The immensely wealthy Sultan Ahmed el-Mansour el Dehbi (the Victorious and Golden) was responsible for building the great pavilions (*koubbas*) in 1591.

Immediately to the left on entering is a pavilion with three chambers. The first is a **Prayer Hall**, with four columns supporting elegant horseshoe arches and a delicately decorative *mihrab* (on the left). This was later pressed into service as a tomb for the six children of Sultan Sidi Mohammed, who died of the plague between 1756 and 1777. The large tomb on the right was the original burial site of the earlier Merenid Sultan Abou Hassan (the Black Sultan), who has since been moved to Rabat.

The central room, the superb **Hall of Twelve Columns**, is the tomb of Ahmed el-Mansour himself, who died of the plague in 1603. His tomb (at the centre) is surrounded by those of his son, grandson (both sultans) and 33 other princes. It is a magnificently sumptuous setting,

lit by a soaring glass dome set into a stucco-laced lantern. The high arched ceiling of carved and gilded cedarwood is supported by a colonnade of 12 Carrara marble columns; the walls and floor are a riot of ceramic tiles and intricately patterned mosaic.

The third small, dark but richly decorated room, the **Hall of Three Niches**, can only be glimpsed from the doorway. In here are the tombs of several wives and children.

In the centre of the courtyard, the **Second Koubba** was built by Ahmed to cover the originally simple tomb of his father, the founder of the dynasty, Mohammed ech Cheikh, who was murdered by Turkish mercenaries in 1557 (his head was salted and taken back to Istanbul as a trophy). Buried with him, in the extravagantly decorative loggia, beneath stalactites of gilded wood, are Ahmed's mother, Lalla Messaouda (in a niche on the right wall), and three other sultans. On the far side of the pavilion is a more simply decorated prayer hall, with *zellij* mosaic and stucco carving.

Palais El Badii (El Badia Palace)

Walk back up Rue Kasbah and turn right. About 600m/656yd along the road, through a small souk, you come to Place des Ferblantiers (tinsmiths), traditionally a metalworkers' quarter, now doubling as a rather chaotic car-park. To your right, go through the Bab Berrima, a huge gateway leading into the double-walled entrance courtyard to **El Badii** (the Incomparable; also one of the 99 names of God). These days it is a ruin, its towering *pisé* (mud and lime) walls home only to copious quantities of chattering storks and pigeons. Let your imagination take you back into the past when it was a palace to rival the greatest in the world, decorated with gold from Guinea,

One of Marrakech's most-visited sites – the Saadian Tombs.

French onyx, Irish granite, Indian and African ivory, snow-white Carrara marble (swapped with Italy for sugar, on a pound for pound basis), mosaics of semi-precious stones, carved cedarwood and lacy stucco, a place of lush gardens and fountain pools, which hosted some of the most extravagant parties in the history of Morocco, according to awed commentators.

Ahmed el-Mansour began work on his new home in 1578, only a few months after the Battle of the Three Kings, using the Portuguese ransoms to fund a lavish building programme and hiring the finest craftsmen from around the world. When the boastful emperor asked his fool his opinion, the fool looked around and replied, 'It will make a grand ruin.'

The words were prophetic. The Badii's days of glory were all too few. In 1696, in his determination to stamp out the Saadian heritage, Alaouite Sultan Moulay Ismaïl stripped it of everything valuable, reusing the pieces in his own new capital in Meknès, and then simply left the rest to rot.

The palace had 360 rooms, surrounding a central court 135m (440ft) long and 110m (360ft) wide. At its centre is a 90m (295ft) long pool, surrounded by four sunken gardens. The pathways above them are actually built over a vast cistern. At one end is the monumental **Koubba El Hamsiniya** (Fifty Pavilion), named in honour of its forest of towering marble columns. Opposite it was the 'Crystal Pavilion'. On the north wall, you can see the last traces of the turquoise tiles from which the 'Green Pavilion' derived its name.

In the northeast corner, you can climb up to a viewing platform. In the southeast corner, in a separate room (additional entrance fee), is the original **minbar** from the Koutoubia, commissioned by Almoravid Sultan Youssef ben

One can only wonder at the splendours that once lay within the formidable walls of the El Badii.

Tachfine in 1137. It has a thousand interlocking pieces of cedar, inlaid with ivory and silver, ebony and sandalwood, which took the finest artisans in Cordoba eight years to create. Next to this, on the south side, the Hayzouran Pavilion, named after the Sultan's favourite wife, is being renovated to house a small museum. Just beyond this is a maze of small rooms and underground passages which included the kitchens, slave quarters and hammams. Beyond these were the private apartments of the Royal family. The Badii is used as the main venue for the annual Marrakech folklore festival.

As you leave the grounds of the Badii and turn right along Rue Berrima, you enter the Marrakech *mellah*. Behind it, cut off from view, is the current **Royal Palace**.

The Mellah

In 1558 Sultan Abdallah el Ghalib set aside
18ha (45 acres) of the medina as a *mellah*
(Jewish district), close to the palace walls to
stress the fact that the Jews, many of whom had
escaped persecution in Spain, were under royal
protection. The sultans found this talented,
sophisticated and generally wealthy group of
people remarkably useful but, in spite of
Islam's supposed religious tolerance, the
Moroccan Jews faced persecution every time

*People, animals
and merchandise
clamour for space in
the mellah souks.*

they strayed outside this carefully guarded district. There are relatively few Jews left but this was also traditionally the centre of the textile, jewellery and spice trade and all three industries are still thriving here today. It is also still the best place in the city for buying spices. On the eastern edge of the *mellah* is a large Jewish cemetery.

On the northern edge of the *mellah*, entered via a narrow, easily overlooked gate and sweet-smelling garden, draped in jasmine and cooled

One of the serene, paved courtyards in the Bahia Palace.

by banana trees, is the **Palais de la Bahia★★** (Bahia Palace, *Rue Riad ez-Zitoun-el-Jdid*), the 19C home of Ba Ahmed, the Vizir to the Alaouite Sultan Moulay Hassan. It later became the French Governor's residence. This is a much grander version of the many riads now being restored to their former glory, with around 150 opulent rooms, brightly painted and elaborately carved cedarwood ceilings, and mosaic-covered and sculpted stucco walls surrounding a labyrinthine series of colonnaded garden courtyards. Only a small portion of the palace, which is still used for official functions, is open to the public.

The Museums

Carry on along Rue Riad ez-Zitoun-el-Jdid. When you reach a small shady square, turn right through Bab Falkten, one of the oldest gates in the city, into Rue Dar Bahia. A short distance along on the right, a narrow doorway leads into the eccentric and fascinating **Maison Tiskiwin★**, a fine old *riad* containing a private museum of Berberian crafts, founded and run by an irascible Dutchman, Bert Flint. If you are lucky, he will show you round. He is an entertaining speaker, has lived in Marrakech for about 40 years and is one of the best guides to the history and anthropology of the region you are likely to find. He is, however, just as likely to be extremely rude and turn his back. With or without his aid, the collection is lively and informative, with wonderful displays of textiles, costumes and jewellery, nomadic and Berber lifestyles.

From here, take the first turning on the right up a little alley to the **Dar Si Saïd et Musée des Art Marocains★★** (Museum of Moroccan Arts

The Museum of Moroccan Arts and Crafts is housed in a fine town palace – worth a visit in its own right.

and Crafts; *closed Tues*), another magnificent 19C mansion, built by Sidi Saïd, chamberlain to Sultan Moulay Hassan and the brother of Grand Vizir Ba Ahmed (who built the Bahia Palace). Where the Tiskiwin concentrates on folk art, this lovely museum is more concerned with the best of Moroccan crafts, with some wonderful wooden carved doors, fine carpets, exquisite filigree jewellery, and a large and varied collection of musical instruments and ornate weaponry.

Stop at a couple of the fine craft galleries in the area before returning to Rue Riad ez-Zitoun-el-Jdid, which leads through a covered souk to Place Jemaa el Fna.

A beautifully inlaid chair – one of the exhibits in the Museum of Moroccan Arts and Crafts.

THE HEART OF THE CITY

Place Jemaa el Fna★★

Laid out as a parade ground by the Almoravids, **Place Jemaa el Fna★★** has been the beating heart of Marrakech since the day the town was founded. Its name means 'Assembly of the Dead' in honour of its past role as the place of public execution, the decapitated heads displayed around the walls. The type of entertainment has changed but **Place Jemaa el Fna at nightfall★★★** becomes a spectacular and irresistable stage.

In the early morning the vast square looks like little more than an overgrown car-park, surrounded to the south by banks and public buildings, but wait a while and watch. There is no better place in the world to rest after hectic sightseeing or shopping, no better excuse to sit on the balcony of a café with a long, cold drink than the ever-changing drama which unfolds at your feet.

The first to arrive are the *calèche* (horse and carriage) and taxi drivers, the vendors of dried fruit and nuts and fresh orange juice, whose permanent stalls fringe the northern edge of the square. Then gradually the first of the buskers arrive. A man puts up an umbrella, lays down a carpet and tips his sleepy snakes out of their basket. Next door, a monkey on a lead is chattering excitedly as a man lays out a herbalist's kit of strange twigs and unmentionable potions. An elderly veiled woman thrusts a pattern book at you, for you to choose your henna tattoo, and a stately bearded man settles himself down cross-legged in an eager ring of listeners to tell a story that will last all day.

As dusk falls on the Place Jemaa el Fna the magic begins.

As the afternoon wears on, the tourists arrive and with them the souvenir sellers. Then, at

The buzz of the crowd as you watch the fire-eaters and acrobats in the crowded Place Jemaa el Fna at night.

Snake charmers (right) and a band of Gnaoua musicians with hypnotic drums (below) attract the crowds in the Place Jemaa el Fna.

five o'clock, as the sun cools and the shadows lengthen, an invisible whistle blows and from every side street pours a crab-like invasion of blue handcarts. Over the next hour, these transform into kitchens and trestle tables. The grills are lit, the menus posted, a pleasing smoky smell of barbecue fills the air, and still the people keep on coming. A troupe of tumblers, gawdy in spangles, a fire-eater, a transvestite belly dancer with a hairy chest, a band of Gnaoua musicians with hypnotic drums, and thousands of people all intent on having a good time.

Keep an eye on your belongings and a pocket full of change for buskers and photographs – usually the crowds are friendly, the food is good, the entertainment dazzling and the evenings warm.

A colourful water-seller (left) and an astrologer (right) offer their services.

43

The Souks★★

On the northern side of the Place Jemaa el Fna are the entrances to the souks – the ultimate Moroccan department store where you can buy everything from diamond rings to donkeys. It is entirely possible to spend whole days in here and get hopelessly lost in the network of alleys. It would take the meanest of misers to come out without spending anything but shopping isn't the only activity. When the souks were first set up in the 11C, each trade was allocated a district and, even today, many of the souks contain workshops. You can choose your lantern accompanied by the clang and hiss of a blacksmith's shop, select the sheepskin for your

Brightly coloured fabrics adorn the Souk des Teinturiers, the dyers' quarter.

custom-made *babouches* (slippers), breathe in
the heady scent of newly cut cedar or
sandalwood and take far too many photos of
drying skeins of wool, newly dyed in bright,
rich colours, ready for the carpet makers.

The main entrance, opposite the Café de
France, leads into a broad street, where
dappled light pours through the bamboo and
iron shades. **Souk Smarine** was traditionally the
home of clothes and textiles, but is well padded
by souvenir shops, pottery and spices these
days. Turn left for some of the most colourful
sections of the souks: the coppersmiths' alley,
Souk des Chaudronniers; carpentry section,
Souk Chouari; blacksmiths in the **Souk**

*Colourful ceramics
to tempt you in the
Souk Smarine.*

Ancient magical remedies for sale in the apothecaries' souk, in Rahba Kédima.

Haddadine; and the gaudily draped dyers' quarter, the **Souk des Teinturiers**. From here you come out onto a small square containing the **Mouassine Mosque and Fountain**, both built in the 1560s by Saadian Sultan Abdallah el Ghalib. The mosque is almost impossible to see in the cramped conditions. The fountain, with three bays (one for people, two for livestock) has suffered from recent 'restoration' and is nothing like as spectacular as it used to be.

Back on Souk Smarine, about 150m/164yd on, a right-hand fork leads to **Rahba Kédima** (apothecaries' souk), formerly the corn market, now a small square of vegetable sellers, herbalists and apothecaries, some full of weird looking dead and dried things with supposedly magical properties, others as pristine as a doctor's surgery, with lines of glass jars and smart men in white coats ready to offer diagnosis and treatment. Also nearby are **Souk Larzal**, home to the wool auctions and a secondhand clothes market; and **Souk Btana**, fortunately no longer given over to odiferous raw skins.

Beyond Rahba Kédima is another small square, Souk Zrabia, more commonly known as **La Criée Berbère** (Berber Auction), now home to a dazzling display of rugs and carpets. Until 1912 this was the site of regular slave auctions (at dusk, each Wednesday, Thursday and Friday), with around 4 000 slaves a year passing through. The 'merchandise' was usually kidnapped in Guinea and Sudan. Prices here were not high – around two slaves for a camel, ten for a horse – prime goods were sold at private viewings.

Back on the main drag, Souk Smarine turns

Carpets are displayed on a shop roof at the Souk Zrabia, where slaves were once auctioned.

into **Souk El Kebir**. Keep going straight and it leads to the *kissarias* (covered markets), home to many of the best, but least photogenic shops, frequented by wealthier Marrakchi. Take the left fork before you get there and you will find yourself in the **Souk Attarin** (spices and perfumes), which leads through to **Souk Smata** (home of the *babouches*).

The entrance to Ben Youssef Medersa, where scholars lived and studied the Koran.

Detail of the ornate zellij and carved plaster decoration in the Ben Youssef Medersa.

Turn right, just before the *kissarias*, for the **Souk des Bijoutiers** (jewellers), and **Souk Cherratin** (leather-workers, carpenters and cobblers). This eventually leads through to the small open space next to the **Ben Youssef Mosque and Medersa★★**.

The first mosque on this site, intended to be the most venerated in the city, was built by Almoravid Sultan Ali ben Youssef in the 12C. The *medersa* (religious school and hostel) opposite was built in the 14C by Merenid Sultan Abou Hassan. In 1562 both were completely rebuilt by Saadian Sultan Abdallah el Ghalib.

The mosque (not open to non-Muslims) shrank in size, while the medersa grew into the splendid affair it is today. At the centre of the complex is a huge, flamboyantly decorated courtyard, with *zellij* mosaic, ornate stucco, and a prayer hall at one end. As many as 900 students at a time were given free lodging for six years in order to study the *Koran* and commentaries. Their rooms surround the courtyard in a series of mini-courts or light-wells, with carved wooden balconies. It remained in use as a religious school until 1962. The mosque was rebuilt again in the 19C.

In its outer courtyard, however, stands the insignificant and easily overlooked **Koubba Ba'Adiyn** (Koubba des Almoravides), a simple domed two-storey pavilion, standing over a washing pool, built by 12C Sultan Ali ben Youssef and the only Almoravid monument left

A huge internal courtyard is at the centre of the Dar M'Nebhi, with museum exhibits in the rooms leading off it.

in Marrakech (*see* p.9). It is easy to see in its architecture, from the horseshoe arches to the decoration of the dome, the pattern on which much of later Moroccan architecture is based.

Just around the corner, in the square, is the privately-owned fine art museum, the **Musée de Marrakech** (*Place Ben Youssef*). The well-displayed collection is worth some time, featuring exhibits by modern Moroccan artists as well as a fine array of older work, including carpets, jewellery, furniture, ceramics, textiles and manuscripts. The house itself is probably the most interesting exhibit. The **Dar M'Nebhi**★ was built in the 19C by the Menebha family, descended from Arab nomads and favourites of the Alaouite Sultans of the period. There is a charming little café in the courtyard which is an ideal place to flop, mid-shop.

THE NORTHERN MEDINA

The northern part of the medina, a largely residential area of winding alleys, home to many of the restored riads which are now offering B&B, is home to a vibrant community, with children playing in the streets, local markets and shops and a way of life virtually untainted by tourism.

There is really only one proper 'sight' in the area. The **Tanneries**★ are best entered from Bab Debbarh, a small city gate in the northeastern corner of the city walls. Hawkers just outside will sell you bunches of fresh mint to ward off the evil smell (a combination of rotting meat and pigeon droppings, which play an important part in the tanning process). It is marginally better early in the morning, before the sun can do its worst; work stops in the afternoons. If you can stand the smell, the tour is fascinating: heaped skins being ladled by sweating men from one vast circular *pisé* pit to

the next, each filled with noxious liquids and rich dyes. It is a glimpse of a medieval trade still being carried on in the same place, using the same techniques.

Watching the tannery workers is a fascinating (though smelly) experience.

There are also numerous mosques in the area (none open to non-Muslims). The 16C **Doukkala Mosque**, in the northwestern corner, was built by Lala Messouada (mother of Ahmed el-Mansour) just inside the **Bab Doukkala**, an imposing 12C Almoravid city gate, now diminished by the main city bus station next door (*see* p.25). Several others are shrines, dedicated to some of the seven saints of Marrakech (*see opposite*). The **Zaouïa of Sidi Bel Abbès** is a huge pyramidal structure, approached through an attractive alley of jewellery stores. The **Zaouïa of Sidi Slimane el-Djazouli** is in a pleasing tangle of small streets with overhead arches, its green-tiled roof barely visible. The only other building of note, the **Dar el Glaoui**, palatial home of Thami el Glaoui (*see* p.63) is unfortunately not open to the public.

The Seven Saints of Marrakech

Like all the best sets of seven saints, Islamic or Christian, these fine men are not dead but simply sleeping; they are the centre of a pilgrimage cult and, as their tombs are scattered across the medina, they are said to guard the city. Their veneration stretches back for centuries. In the 18C Sultan Moulay Ismaïl gave them all nice new shrines and instituted an official seven-day *moussem* (pilgrimage).

Sidi Bel Abbès (born in Ceuta in 1130) was a hermit invited to live in Marrakech by Sultan Yacoub el Mansour, who set up a whole collection of schools, hostels and poor houses, some of which are still supported today. He is the patron of the city and guardian of merchants, peasants and the blind.

Mohammed ben Slimane el-Djazouli was a famous 15C Sufi mystic and a leader of the *jihad* against Portugal; **Sidi Youssef ben Ali** was the protector of lepers; **Sidi Abdallah el Ghezouani** was a hermit who prophesied the downfall of decadent Fès and died in 1528; **Imam Assouheili** was an intellectual from Spain. The others are **Sidi Abd el Aziz**, who died in 1508; and **Sidi Ayad**, at whose shrine the *moussem* traditionally begins.

The tomb of Sidi Bel Abbès.

CITY WALLS** AND GARDENS

The Walls**

The earliest city wall was a simple stockade of camel thorn. In 1126-27 Ali ben Youssef replaced this with high *pisé* walls built of mud and lime, with a crenellated walkway around the top. Over the centuries these same 9m/10ft-high walls have been patched, mended and rebuilt and still surround the medina today. Altogether they are around 10km (6 miles) long, with about 200 towers and 15 gates. It is worth doing a circuit – the traditional way is to hire a *calèche* (horse and carriage) in the late afternoon. A bicycle is a good alternative. Few of the gates are of real interest, and many have been opened up or by-passed in order to allow modern traffic to move freely.

Backed by gaunt palms and dramatic mountain scenery, the crenellated city walls.

Sitting back in a horse-drawn calèche *and watching the city walls turn to gold in the late afternoon light.*

Tour the walls with a leisurely calèche ride.

The Gardens

Marrakech has five gardens, all of which are worth a visit, although few of them match what we would consider to be the usual mix of grass, trees and flowers. The closest are the **Mamounia Gardens**, only open to hotel guests (*see* p.85).

In the far south of the medina, next to the Royal Palace, are the **Jardin de l'Aguedal★** (Aguedal Gardens; *about 4km/2.5 miles from Place Jemaa el Fna; open Friday afternoon and Sunday only; closed if the Royal family is in residence*), founded in the 12C by Sultan Abd el-Moumen as the palace farm. Two vast irrigation tanks, filled with water channelled down from Ourika, are surrounded by huge orchards of olives, citrus figs, pomegranates and apricots. In the 19C the gardens were

restored and various sultans added pleasure pavilions. Sultan Sidi Mohammed drowned in the largest of the pools in 1873, when his steam launch capsized.

The **Jardin de la Ménara** (Menara Gardens; *2km/1 mile east of the medina, just beyond Guéliz*), is also very much a working plantation of around 30 000 olive trees, originally laid out around a huge irrigation tank by the 12C Almohads but redesigned by the Alaouites in

Bright Mediterranean blue, lush greenery and cooling pools feature in the designer Majorelle Garden.

the 19C. They are a favourite picnic spot for Marrakchi families, with wonderful views across the city to the High Atlas mountains.

Probably the most spectacular garden is the relatively small (5ha/12 acre) **Jardin Majorelle**★★ (Majorelle Garden; *just off Av. Yacoub el Mansour*) in a smart residential district to the north of the new city. Created by French painter, Jacques Majorelle, who lived in Marrakech from 1922 until his death in 1962, then bought by Yves Saint-Laurent, these fabulous gardens hold an important plant collection but are also a work of art. Lily ponds and fountains, bamboo groves, palms and cascades of bougainvillea contrast starkly with the sculptural qualities of giant cacti, all framed by vivid cobalt blue buildings. Owing to numerous appearances on gardening shows, the Majorelle Garden has become one of the key influences in modern garden design. The

Taking a break in the Palmeraie.

building at the centre houses Yves Saint-Laurent's small **Museum of Islamic Art** (separate entrance fee), including a collection of Majorelle's paintings.

The last and biggest of the gardens is the **Palmeraie**, a vast 13 000ha (32 000 acres) estate planted with around 150 000 rather neglected, under-irrigated but very picturesque date palms, supposedly laid out in the 11C by Youssef ben Tachfine as a vital food source. These days the area, to the northeast of the city, has also become 'millionaire's row', its expensive hotels and golf courses interspersed with enormous family mansions. There is an attractive 8km (5 mile) circular drive through the district that makes an excellent *calèche* or cycle ride.

GUÉLIZ (NEW TOWN)

This is a far cry from the atmospheric chaos of the medina. The new town, Guéliz, was laid out by French architect Henri Prost in the 1920s and takes its name from a corruption of the French word *église*. One of the first and most important buildings was the **Catholic Church of the Holy Martyrs** – one of the few Christian churches in Marrakech, now joined by a synagogue and a mosque.

The new town has a clear grid system, wide boulevards and lots and lots of very ordinary buildings. This is the working centre of town, with banks and offices, useful shops, travel agents, apartment blocks and hotels. It is worth a quick look round and perhaps a stop at one of the excellent restaurants and pâtisseries (*see* pp. 98, 101) but there really isn't much to hold the sightseer's attention.

The main road, linking up with the medina next to the Koutoubia, is **Av. Mohammed V**, where you will find most of the useful shops.

The broad Avenue Mohammed V leads from the medina to Guéliz.

Just north of Place du 16 Novembre there is a **covered market**, selling mainly fruit and vegetables, with a friendly neighbourhood atmosphere. A little further up is Place Abdel Moumen ben Ali, the home of the tourist office and a couple of excellent cafés.

The **Palais de Congrès** (*Av. de France*) is the very successful Marrakech conference centre. West of the ramparts running north from Bab Jdid is the pleasant garden suburb of **Hivernage**. With a backdrop of the city walls and planted with mature trees and gardens, this area of splendid villas and hotels makes a refreshing and relaxing place for a quiet stroll.

EXCURSIONS FROM MARRAKECH

THE ROAD TO OUARZAZATE★★

Although only 196km (122 miles), the drive from Marrakech to Ouarzazate takes 4-5 hours because of the twisting mountain roads. It can be done as a long day trip but it is better to stay one or two nights and use Ouarzazate as a base for exploring the Drâa and Dadès Valleys. Check before travelling in winter, as the road is frequently blocked by snow.

The main road from Marrakech to Ouarzazate, built by the French in 1936, has 803 hairpin bends (according to one local). The scenery is utterly magnificent, every bend opening up a new vista of plunging valleys, snow-capped peaks and spectacular lighting effects. The high point of the route, **Tizi-n-Tichka★★**, is 2 260m (7 415ft) above sea level, a howling, windswept place which separates the lush,

The drive to Ouarzazate provides stunning views and dramatic scenery, such as the valley of the river Mellah from Âït-Benhaddou.

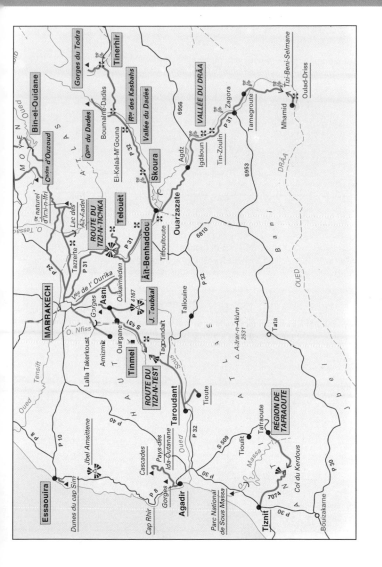

A Berber village sits high on the Tizi-n-Tichka pass.

tightly terraced, northern slopes from the ochre desert rocks to the south. Everywhere are rickety Berber villages, ruinous kasbahs, and stalls offering crystals and fossils for sale.

Four kilometres beyond Tizi-n-Tichka, keep a sharp lookout for the turning to the **Kasbah of Telouèt** – it is not obvious. From the main road, it is 21km (13 miles) to the overwhelmingly powerful, blood-red kasbah that was the seat of the Glaoui family, whose name means 'Lion of the Atlas'. In the late 19C they rose to be paramount chiefs of the southern regions; by the mid-20C they were kingmakers When the French built the new road across the mountains, they deliberately bypassed the kasbah in the hope of containing

Left: The village of Telouèt is guarded by the ruined kasbah, once the palace of the powerful Glaoui tribe.

Right: The village of Telouèt, seen from the kasbah.

the Glaoui family's activities – to little effect.

In 1953 Thami el Glaoui, the pro-French pasha (governor) of Marrakech, was one of a group of nationalist leaders who decided that the sultan, who had nationalist leanings, had to go. The sultan was sent into exile. In 1955, amid growing political chaos, he requested the sultan's return. The sultan duly returned but El Glaoui himself was disgraced and his family stripped of their possessions. The kasbah is now a magnificent labyrinthine ruin. There are guides present to take you round the few sections of the building still safe to visit.

From here there are two routes to Âït-Benhaddou. If you have a 4x4, take the wonderful 35km (22 miles) route across the mountains. If you have a normal car,

return to the main road and continue south; about 30km (19 miles) before you reach Ouarzazate, turn left and continue for 15km (9 miles).

The reason people stop at **Aït-Benhaddou★★** is to see one of the most dramatically beautiful and easily accessible of the ruined kasbahs, a powerful control on the trade routes since the 16C. More recently it has been used by several film makers including Orson Wells (*Sodom and Gomorrah* and *Jesus of Nazareth*) and David Lean (*Lawrence of Arabia*). It has been designated a UNESCO World Heritage sight. Money has been allocated for its restoration but so far little has happened. The tiny village has a couple of small hotels and cafés, and a row of souvenir shops.

Local Berber carpets are the speciality at Ouarzazate.

Return to the main road and carry on to long, skinny modern **Ouarzazate**, founded as a garrison town by the French in the 1920s. This has also been used as a film set by numerous directors, including Bertolucci, who filmed parts of *The Sheltering Sky* in the area. At the **Studios Atlas**, on the outskirts, you can visit various film sets. The town is also a useful base, with plenty of hotels, tour operators and travel agents offering a wide variety of tours of the nearby valleys.

At the far end of town, the imposingly tall and decorative **Kasbah Taourirt★★** (*open daily 8am-6.30pm*) was built by the Glaouis to protect their southern trade routes. Today, however, the vast majority of the old walled town is fenced off and only the citadel is open to the public. It is worth taking a guided tour through a few of the more decorative state rooms of the rambling mud-built tower.

Across the road, the **Centre Artisanal** has an interesting collection of craft shops and a couple of good restaurant-cafés.

Another Glaoui Kasbah, **Tiffoultoute★**, 7km (4 miles) beyond the town, is now a hotel-restaurant but also offers guided tours.

The high mountain pass between the Dadès Gorge and the Todra Gorge – a dramatic and powerful landscape.

THE KASBAH TRAIL★★

From Ouarzazate, two long valleys cut across the desert flatlands. Both are lavishly strewn with kasbahs and oases, providing wonderful trekking country and spectacular scenic surroundings.

Vallée du Dadès★★ (Dadès Valley)

The **Dadès Valley★★** rambles roughly east, the river forcing its way through a stark, imposing landscape in which mud-built kasbahs in varying states of disrepair meld organically into the jumble of volcanic rock. The **El Mansour Eddhabi Barrage** is a 30km- (18 mile) long reservoir used to irrigate thousands of hectares of palm groves and fruit orchards. A little way further on is the attractive little agricultural town of **Skoura★★**, and 50km (31 miles) beyond that you reach the **El-Kelaâ M'Gouna★** (Valley of Roses), famous for its roses, home to a May rose festival and a thriving industry in rose water. Continue for another 24km (15 miles) to **Boumalne** and the entrance to

El-Kelaâ M'Gouna, one of the kasbahs in the Dadès Valley, is noted for its rose-water production.

the **Dadès Gorge★★**, where a switchback roller-coaster of a road meanders up and down the sides of a towering, almost impossibly romantic, canyon filled with almond trees and kasbahs. Back in Boumalne, another much easier route leads for 53km (33 miles) to **Tinerhir★★**, a popular tourist town ringed by high peaks with a thriving rug-making industry. It marks the entrance to the **Gorges du Todra★★** (Todra Gorge), a massive, 1 000m (3 280ft) deep fault line, with a road along the bottom.

The picturesque Dadès Gorge is dotted with villages perched precariously on the canyon sides.

The Drâa Valley★★★

After climbing over the 1 660m (5 450ft) Tizi-n-Tinififft pass, the road beside the Drâa River gorge winds south for 68km (42 miles) through dry and dusty hills to the oasis town of **Agdz**, circled by palm groves and hung with rugs for the tourists. From here the valley widens and the river becomes an extended oasis, slicing through the Saharan sands, the precious fields and water guarded from the predations of the desert nomads by some 50 heavily fortified

A spice trader, in an open-air souk in the Drâa Valley.

ksour, including **Ksar Tamnougalt** (6km/3.7 miles from Agdz) and the dramatic medieval **Kasbah Timiderte** (8km/5 miles further).

Zagora began life as a crossroads for camel caravans, became the administrative centre of the Drâa and is now a starting point for camel safaris. It has markets on Sunday and Wednesday. Twelve kilometres (7 miles) further south, the small walled city of **Tamegroute★** is home to the **Zaouia Nassiriya**, a religious centre since the 17C, with a priceless library of Koranic manuscripts. **Mhamid** is the nearest place to get deep into the desert dunes.

Kasbahs and Ksour

The word *kasbah* conjures up romantic images of desert warriors and harems but what actually does it mean? Simply a Moroccan castle. A fortified village, often clustered at the foot of the castle, is known as a *ksar* (plural *ksour*).

During much of Morocco's history, the country has been split into small warring principalities and brigand territories, and the formidable fortifications were both a statement of intent and necessary to survival. The southern slopes of the High Atlas are littered with kasbahs and ksour, piled like lego bricks up the steep slopes.

Built from the local earth, they merge organically into the hillside, only their crenellations and the geometric patterns on the towers standing proud. The grander kasbahs would have whitewashed windows, while inside they had ornately painted wooden ceilings.

Like those of medieval Europe, the castles were strategically placed to guard the mountain passes and trade routes. Often no more than a few kilometres apart, they ensured that no enemy could invade nor camel caravan creep through without paying its tolls. Most of the kasbahs are now derelict, although some are returning to life as hotels and restaurants.

While the lords in their castles were definitely in charge, day-to-day life in the villages was run on semi-communal lines, with a council made up of the

heads of families, the *jamaa*. Each family had its own courtyard house but there were also many communal buildings, including wells, sheep pens, grain stores, meeting halls, the mosque and a school. People still live in many of the villages today, patching the crumbling mud walls with corrugated iron and plastic.

Right: Berber children, Imlil.
Below: Âït-Benhaddou.

OURIKA AND OUKAÏMEDEN★

Leave Marrakech on the S513. Souk Tnine de l'Ourika is just off the main road, 30km (18 miles) from the city; Setti-Fatma is 37km (23 miles) further on.

One of the most popular organised tours from Marrakech is to the large and now very touristy **Souk Tnine de l'Ourika** (Monday morning), at the edge of a bustling market town, whose river banks are turned into a vast donkey park for the duration. The locals are well-versed in all the ploys to rid tourists of their *dirhams* but it is worth it for the colour, the razzmatazz and the photo opportunities (payment usually required).

From here the **Ourika Valley★** cuts deep into the heart of the High Atlas, the road straggling through a series of small hamlets for around

Remote and at times inhospitable, a Berber village in the Ourika Valley.

40km (24 miles) to **Setti-Fatma**, a large, modern village surrounded on three sides by towering peaks. A short but strenuous scramble from the village is a series of seven waterfalls (wear shoes with ankle supports and a good grip).

Half way along the valley, before you get to Setti-Fatma, a road on the right climbs up through the clouds along dizzyingly precipitous roads to **Oukaïmeden★**, Morocco's premier ski resort (3 273m/10 740 ft). It has a chairlift up to good piste and off-piste skiing, if the snow arrives, which is not always the case. The village overlooks a small lake and ring of snow-capped hills and is an excellent place in summer for wild flowers, herbs, orchids and birds. There are also a number of prehistoric **rock paintings** and engravings in the area.

Oukaïmeden – tranquil in summer, a playground for skiers in winter.

ASNI AND TIZI-N-TEST★★★

*Asni is 47km (29 miles) south of Marrakech on the
S501 to Taroudant, while Ouirgane is 13km
(8 miles) further on. Tizi-n-Test is a further 74km
(46 miles).*

Asni is a small Berber town, tucked into a
sheltered valley, with two claims to fame. One is
as a trekking centre, the other as the site of a
large Sunday market, though smaller and
much less touristy than Ourika. The emphasis
is definitely on vegetables rather than souvenirs
(though you can buy these as well), while the
whole souk is bathed in the smell of barbecued
lamb. As fascinating as the souk itself, is
watching the laden donkeys arriving and
departing, a Berber man perched precariously
on the huge sacks of produce. Traditionally,
only the men went to market – the women
couldn't even go shopping, although this is
changing now.

From Asni a rough 17km (10.5 mile) track
leads up to **Imlil**, while the main road heads

*The relaxed and
attractive town of
Imlil is an ideal base
for trekking into the
Toubkal National
Park and High Atlas.*

south to **Ourigane**, a charmingly sited village with a couple of good hotels – the very smart Roseraie and the pleasantly affordable Sanglier Qui Fume (*see* p.93). This makes an excellent base for some gentle mountain walking, riding or trekking in the Nfiss Gorges.

Further on, the village of **Ijoukak** has some of the most beautiful scenery in the High Atlas and some wonderful walks to ancient monuments. The 12C **Tinmel Mosque★★** (8km/5 mile walk) is the only mosque in the region which non-Muslims are permitted to enter and the last remnant of the city that gave birth to the Almohad dynasty. Six kilometres south of Ijoukak is the village of **Talat-N-Yâkcoub**, with a ruined kasbah and entertaining Wednesday souk.

There are breathtaking views from the Tizi-n-Test pass, one of the highest in Morocco.

Beyond here the road continues to climb up to the magnificently savage **Tizi-n-Test★★** pass (2 100m/6 900ft), from where there are breathtaking views (if not obscured by the frequent mountain mists).

TREKKING IN THE HIGH ATLAS^^^

Trekking has become one of the most popular pastimes in the Moroccan Atlas. The terrain is ideal – high, remote and beautiful but never so high or cut off that you are out of touch with safety. All but a few small areas are easily accessible to reasonably fit people and all along the way, small villages add a touch of entertainment and evening hospitality. It is also possible to find more strenuous climbs and canyons.

The summer trekking season is from April to October, although you should head high in mid-summer to escape the heat. There are occasional violent summer storms. Winter ski-trekking is possible from February to the end of April. In all cases it is advisable to hire a licensed mountain guide and a baggage mule or porters. You can find them in most of the mountain villages, at the Hotels Ali and Foucauld in Marrakech, or through specialist tour operators (*see* p.109).

Asni is the main trekking centre for the High Atlas while **Imlil** is the starting point for the Toubkal massif, which at 4 167m (13 670ft) is the highest point in North Africa. Allow at least three days, preferably more, to acclimatise to the altitude (most organised treks take 5-10 days). Between Asni and Imlil and between Imlil and **Setti-Fatma** there are several excellent lower altitude walks which will satisfy those pressed for time or who are less ambitious.

For detailed advice, read *Trekking in the Moroccan Atlas*, by Rich Knight (published by Trailblazer).

A High Atlas valley, near Asni.

CASCADES D'OUZOUD★★
(OUZOUD CASCADES)

202km (126 miles) northeast of Marrakech. Allow up to 3hrs each way. Take the P24 out of town towards Béni Mellal; after about 160km (100 miles), turn right at the sign for Cascades d'Ouzoud. The falls are 21km (13 miles) further on.

These magnificent waterfalls, 110m (350ft) high and made up of around 25 small falls, tumble over the cliff in stages, each narrower than the last, decoratively framed by twisted rock formations and climbing plants. There are a number of small watermills at the top. At the bottom of the deep canyon is a series of pools which are wonderful for a cooling swim (be careful of high water and strong currents). Keep an eye out for the macaques, highly endangered apes with beige fur. There are a couple of small hotels and cafés.

An alternative route to the cascades, along the S508 to Azilal, is very scenic and takes you through the small walled town of Demnate, which has a large Sunday souk, and has good views of the **Bin-el-Ouidane lake★★**, formed by a dam.

ESSAOUIRA★★

On the coast, 171km (108 miles) from Marrakech. It is an easy 2hr drive, on a good road. Most of the old city is pedestrianised; there is a car-park near the port.

Half way to Essaouira you will see the famous tree-climbing goats, who are supposedly so passionate about argan nuts that they have learned to scramble into the trees in search of them. For about a kilometre, the trees on either side of the road are beset by rather startled high-altitude goats, while their shepherds concentrate on collecting tips from the tourists.

Essaouira is an enchantingly pretty walled

Essaouira's colourful port.

blue and white town, now rapidly succumbing to mass tourism, its 6km-long crescent of golden sand filling up with monolithic resort hotels and a newly equipped international airport. The offshore islands give some protection against Atlantic waves but high spring and autumn winds can whip up the sea and bring the surfers out in force. They also keep summer temperatures significantly cooler than inland.

The town began life in the 7C BC as the Phoenician trading port of Thamusida. By the 1C BC, under the rule of King Juba II of Mauretania, cargoes gathered from across north and west Africa included ostrich feathers, salt, spices, shad, cereals, horses, gold dust, textiles, and the rich purple dye harvested from murex shellfish and coveted by the Romans as Imperial purple. By the 11C it was the largest port in southern Morocco and

sugar cane, slaves and piracy had joined the list of profitable cargoes. In 1506 it was seized by the Portuguese, who renamed it Mogador, but recaptured in 1541 by the Saadians, who then ignored it in favour of Agadir.

In 1760 Alaouite Sultan Mohammed ben Abdallah decided to humble rebellious Agadir. He commissioned French engineer, Theodore Cornue, to design the new city of Essaouira ('little ramparts'), based on Vauban's plan of St Malo. It was officially 'opened' in 1769. The grid of wide streets inside imposing walls is the only planned town in Morocco and has few signs of Islamic architecture. The sultan then signed commercial agreements with several European nations and the fledgling American colonies. Within a few years Essaouira's new, all-year port was handling over 40 percent of Morocco's maritime trade.

Since then container ships have left the little port far behind, a picturesque backwater beloved of artists. Orson Welles came here to film *Othello* (the town now has a square and monument in his honour); Jimi Hendrix and the Rolling Stones were amongst the 1960s influx of hippies. Today, some of Morocco's finest artists still have their studios here. Best amongst the many galleries is **Galerie d'Art Frédéric Damgaard** (*Av. Oqba-Ibn-Nafiaâ*).

There are few actual sights. The **port★**, still Morocco's third largest sardine fishing port, is a colourful tangle of nets and buoys, boat repair yards, fish markets and seafood restaurants. Along one side of the walls is the **Skala of the Kasbah★**, a wide gun platform lined by ornamental but very business-like cannons, originally cast for Philip II of Spain and given to the sultan by 19C traders, flanked by a squat round tower. Below the ramparts is a fascinating line of thuja (evergreen coniferous tree) carpenters' workshops; this is the centre of the finest woodwork in Morocco (*see* p.103). In the centre of town, in a 19C pasha's residence, is the **Musée Sidi Mohammed ben Abdallah** (*Derb Laâlouj; normally open 9.30am-12.30pm. 2.30-6.30pm, closed Tues; currently closed for restoration*). It has a fine collection of local arts, crafts, musical instruments and carpets.

Wander from here through the maze of **souks★**, haggling for carpets or thuja work, to the main square, **Place Moulay el Hassan**, where you will find plenty of cafés, street traders and entertainers. Next to this, the ornamental 18C **Porte de la Marine★** leads through to the port.

The **Îles Purpuraires** are now a bird sanctuary, the breeding site of Eleonora's falcon. Visits are strongly discouraged and require a permit.

The day's catch is prepared for the fish market, Essaouira.

THE SPIRIT OF MARRAKECH

The spirit of Marrakech lives in the shadowy alleys and high faceless walls of the medina and in the broad, brash boulevards of the modern city, where men gather in tea houses to comment on the world in a haze of rough tobacco smoke. It lives in the raucous salesmanship of the souks, in the monk-like figures in their hooded robes, sheltering from the excess of the summer sun, and the suave young men in leather jackets who like nothing better than to flirt extravagantly.

It lives in the women, some shrouded in black veils, some in jeans and skimpy t-shirts, many with a compromise headscarf tucked around their chins. It lives in the boys, who practise drumming and football late into the evening, and in the girls, who earnestly follow their mothers as they do the household chores. It lives in the sinuous dancers of the Jemaa el Fna, who turn out, on close inspection, to be men in drag. It lives in the street stalls and cafés, in the elegant restaurants with their mosaic walls and fountain courtyards, in a glass of

fresh orange juice and the scent of a steaming *tajine* as the lid is lifted with a flourish.

Above all, it is a spirit of almost overwhelming hospitality, a gracious, gentle and utterly sincere welcome from a people who love, above all, to entertain their honoured guests.

WEATHER

In many ways Marrakech has an ideal climate, with low humidity and plenty of sunshine all year. The small amount of rainfall is fairly evenly spread from October to April.

Midwinter can be cool, with a midday temperature of 18-20°C dropping to a chilly 4-6°C overnight. Summer is searingly hot, with midday temperatures routinely at 39-40°C. The ideal times to visit are from March to April and from October to November, with the midday temperature at a balmy 23-28°C, dropping to 10-12°C at night.

Even during the height of summer, the High Atlas mountains, just south of the city, keep cool and fresh, while in winter

Laughing, flirting and haggling over the carpet of your dreams and a glass of mint tea.

there is usually enough snow to ski. The coastal area around Essaouira is milder in winter and cooler in summer, the temperature modulated by the Canaries current which also brings occasional summer cloud and fog.

CALENDAR OF EVENTS

2nd Sunday in January:
Marrakech International Marathon

March:
Festival of Moulay Aissa ben Idriss in Beni-Mellal (in the High Atlas, east of Marrakech)

End of May:
Festival of Roses in El Kelaâ M'Gouna (Dadès Valley)

Early June:
10-day Festival of Folk Arts in Marrakech (hugely entertaining and colourful national popular arts festival)

Mid-Late June:
3-day Festival of Essaouira (Gnaoua folk and world music)

End August:
3-day Festival in Setti-Fatma (Ourika Valley, south of Marrakech)

End September:
Festival of Sidi Moussa ou Quarqour (near Kelaat-Seraghna, north of Marrakech)

3rd week of September:
Bethrothal Festival in Imilchil (Middle Atlas, east of Marrakech)

October:
International Film Festival in Marrakech

Music, colour and joy blend in the traditional marriage festival, Imilchil.

Moveable festivals to commemorate the 'Aid Al Mouloud' (in celebration of the Prophet's birthday): Moulay Ibrahim Festival (road to Asni, 50km/31 miles southwest of Marrakech), in the 2nd week following the 'Aid Al Mouloud'; and El Aouina Festival (18km/11 miles southwest of Marrakesh), one month after the 'Aid Al Mouloud'

ACCOMMODATION

Most of the larger, 3-5 star tourist hotels are in the new town; they are comfortable but uninspiring, with gardens, pools, a couple of restaurants and a bar. Three names stand out: the grand, historic Mamounia, the exquisitely designed Amanjena and the vast Palmeraie Golf Palace resort.

The best of the smaller hotels are clustered near Place Jemaa el Fna, in the medina. Facilities are basic but rooms are clean; the hotels are well situated and very, very cheap.

There is also a rapidly growing collection of delightful small B&Bs *maisons d'hôtes*, few with more than nine rooms, most in the medina, which range in price from moderate to very expensive (*see* p.88).

Prices
(based on a double room, with breakfast, per night):
Inexpensive: up to 400DH
Moderate: 400-900DH
Expensive: 900-1500DH
Very Expensive: above 1500DH

Recommendations

Top of the range hotels (in town)

Hotel Es Saâdi *Av. El-Quadissia, Hivernage*
☎ **04-444 8811/444 7010**
fax: 04-444 7644
web: www.essaadi.com
Well-situated near Place 16 Novembre, in Guéliz, this large 5-star hotel has comfortable, well-furnished rooms, tennis courts, hammam, a good French restaurant, small casino and fine pool. Very expensive.

Hotel Kenzi Semiramis *Route de Casablanca, Quartier Semlalia, BP 525* ☎ **04-443 1377**
fax. 04-444 7127

Large, luxurious 5-star resort hotel on the outskirts of the new city, with four restaurants, disco and karaoke, good sports facilities and spacious, comfortable rooms. Popular with tour groups. Pool. The same chain runs the 5-star Farah Hotel in Guéliz. Very expensive.

La Mamounia *Av. Bab Jdid*
☎ **04-444 4409**
fax: 04-444 4660
web: www.mamounia.com
A landmark and sight as well as the grandest hotel in Marrakech, the wonderful, 5-star de luxe La Mamounia is the only large hotel inside the medina; it has a fascinating mix of Moroccan and art deco décor, three superb restaurants (international, Italian and

The gardens and pool at La Mamounia hotel, Marrakech.

Moroccan) and a casino. It also has the finest gardens in the city. Pool. Very expensive.

Hotel Nassim *115 Av. Mohammed V, Guéliz* ☎ **04-444 6401** fax: 04-443 6710
Comfortable if uninspired 4-star hotel, a couple of minutes' walk from the tourist office. Decorated in marble, leather and glass, with a piano bar, international restaurant, terrace and small pool. Excellent value for money. Moderate.

Méridien N'Fis *Av. de France* ☎ **04-433 9400/444 8772** fax: 04-444 7446
web: www.lemeridien-hotels.com
Large, comfortable business-style hotel, with Mediterranean and international restaurants, a bar, pool and attractive 5ha gardens. Very expensive.

Sheraton *Av. de la Menara, BP 528* ☎ **04-444 8998/443 8111** fax: 04-443 7843
web: www.starwoodhotels.co
As comfortable and luxurious as is usual for this huge international chain, with a splendid lobby ceiling, but bland international architecture elsewhere. Three good restaurants – international buffet, pizzeria and Moroccan – a bar, tennis courts and huge pool. Expensive.

Hotel Meliá Tichka *Route de Casablanca, Quartier Semlalia BP 894* ☎ **04-444 8710** fax: 04-444 8691
web: www.solmelia.com

Next to the Semiramis, on the northern outskirts of the new city. The 4-star Tichka is famed for its bold, if slightly tired décor, designed by Bill Willis, a Marrakech-based American who has become the local style guru, using nothing but Moroccan materials. Pool. Expensive.

La Maison Arabe *1 Derb Assehbe, Rue Bab Doukkala, Medina* ☎ **04-438 7010** fax: 04-438 7221
web: www.lamaisonarabe.com
One of the first hotels to be created from a historic house in the medina, this is a charmingly decorated and smoothly-run establishment, centred on two flower-filled courtyards, but with definite hotel anonymity rather than the cosiness of a *maison d'hôte*. It has a pool (10 minutes away by shuttle), a Moroccan restaurant and runs courses in Moroccan cookery. Very expensive.

Villa des Orangers *6 Rue Sidi Mimoun, Medina* ☎ **04-438 4638**; fax: 04-438 5123
web: www.villadesorangers.com
Small, full-service 5-star hotel in two beautiful old *riads*, with impeccably and delightfully decorated public rooms and courtyards, spacious well-appointed rooms, some with private terraces, and a small pool on the roof. Well situated between Place Jemaa el Fna and the Badii Palace. Very expensive.

Smaller Hotels

Hotel Central Palace *59 Derb Sidi Bouloukat, Medina* ☎ **04-444 0235**
fax: 04-444 2844
Cheap, cheerful, clean and very convenient, just off Place Jemaa el Fna. Will change money and rent bikes. Inexpensive.

Hotel Foucauld *Rue el Mouahidine, Medina* ☎ **04-444 5499**
fax: 04-444 1344
Small, simple, reliable hotel near the Koutoubia. Used as a trekking base, so full of eager outdoorsy types. International restaurant. Inexpensive.

Hotel Oudaya *147 Rue Mohammed El Bekal, Guéliz*
☎ **04-444 8512** fax: 04-443 5400
Friendly 3-star hotel, in a quiet residential area. The bedrooms are a little small but the hotel is attractively designed by Charles Boccara, with a Moroccan theme. International and Moroccan restaurants and pool. Some rooms with balconies and/or air-conditioning (for a premium). Moderate.

Hotel Tazi *corner Rue Bab Agnaou and Rue El Mouahidine, Medina*
☎ **04-444 2787** fax: 04-444 2152
Well-situated, rather faded, family run hotel with comfortable rooms, a bar and pool (both open to non-residents). Inexpensive.

Le Gallia *30 Rue de la Recette, Medina* ☎ **04-444 5913**
fax: 04-444 4853
Well situated, only 500m/547yd from Place Jemaa el Fna, this attractive, simple hotel has been in operation since 1929, a forerunner of the *riads*, with 19 rooms arranged around two charming garden courtyards. Book ahead – it is very popular. Inexpensive.

Riads
Riad agencies
All these agencies will find you bed and breakfast or a whole *riad* to rent. They will also help you buy and restore your own *riad*, if you become addicted.

Best of Morocco *Seend, Wilts SN12 6NZ* ☎ **01380-828 533**
fax: 01380-828 630
web: www.morocco-travel.com
Specialist UK operator with encyclopaedic knowledge, organising hotel stays and tailor-made tours, with a fine list of hotels and *riads*.

Marrakech-Riads *8 Derb Charfa Lakbir, Mouassine 4000, Marrakech* ☎ **04-438 5858** fax: 04-438 5708
web: www.marrakech-riads.net
Small but growing collection of delightfully simple *riads* owned by

Relaxing in the sun on the roof terrace of a riad, *as the muezzin flood the city with the evening call to prayer.*

a charming Moroccan man, Abdellatif Aït ben Abdallah, one of the prime movers behind the restoration of the medina. These small *riads* can be hired as B&B or as a whole house. Other meals available on request.

Marrakech-Medina *102 Rue Dar el-Pacha* ☎ **04-444 9133**
fax: 04-439 1071
web: marrakech-medina.com
Reputable agency specialising in the rental of whole houses, with a range of properties sleeping 2-15 people.

Individual properties

There are over 300 **maisons d'hôtes** in the medina. This is just a small selection.

Dar Atta *28 Rue R'mila Derb Rouia, Medina* ☎ **04-438 6232**
fax: 04-438 6241
web: www.cybernet.net.ma/daratta
Attractively decorated and furnished *riad*, excellently situated near Bab Ksour, with ten rooms, an open courtyard and two sun terraces. Also has a hammam, craft shop and offers massages. Moderate-expensive.

Dar El Farah *Arset Bouachrine, Riad-ez-Zitoun-el-Jdid, Medina* ☎ **04-443 1560** fax: 04-443 1559
e-mail: riadmedina@cybernet.net.ma
Eight individual and stylishly decorated bedrooms, around a courtyard with a small swimming pool, well situated near the Bahia Palace. Access through the adjacent garden. Car parking.

Also takes bookings for several other *riads*. Expensive.

Dar Nejna *18 Douar Graoua, Rue Tikhezrit* ☎ **04-437 7379**
fax: 04-444 5260
Next to the Lycée Mohammed V. French-run, comfortable and friendly, but a little too European and a little too far off the beaten track for a true Arabian Nights fantasy. Moderate.

Riad Catalina *21 Derb Abdellah ben Hessaein* ☎ **04-442 6701**
fax: 04-442 6702
web: www.riadcatalina.com
Beautifully restored and superbly located at Bab Ksour (Gate of the Palaces), a few minutes' walk from Place Jemaa el Fna, with exactly the right balance of Moroccan splendour and European comfort. Small swimming pool on the roof. Expensive.

Riad Enija *Rahba Lakdima, 9 Derb Mesfioui*
☎ **04-444 0926/0014**
fax: 04-444 2700
web: www.riadenija.com
A magnificent fantasy property, run by a German-Swedish couple, in the heart of the souk, with nine rooms around two courtyards. The buildings are beautifully restored but what sets this extra-ordinary *riad* apart is the bold décor, matching traditional Moroccan style with ultra-modern furnishings to dazzling visual effect. Small pool on the roof. Very expensive.

Shady pavilions and tranquil waters at the Amanjena Resort hotel.

Villa Oasis *Quartier Arset el Baraka Derb el Makina Bab Aïlen, Medina* ☎ **04-438 8008** fax: 04-438 7777
This attractive *riad*, in the south-eastern corner of the medina, has the classic Moroccan-style court-yard with a swimming pool in the centre. Its six rooms are extremely well appointed with satellite TV, a phone and fridge, giving it more the feeling of a hotel than a B&B. Massages and a hammam available. Very expensive.

Just Outside Marrakech

Amanjena Resort *Post principale de Guéliz, Marrakech 40 000, BP 2405* ☎ **04-440 3353** fax: 04-440 3477 web: www.amanresorts.com
A sumptuous resort hotel on the edge of the Palmeraie. Each of its very spacious 40 rooms is a separate pavilion with its own gazebo and garden. With acres of water gardens, two superb restau-rants (Moroccan and European), a library and bar, all immaculately designed and oozing luxury, this is the perfect relaxing hideaway for the very rich. Very expensive.

Caravan Serai *Ouled ben Rahmoun* ☎ **04-443 6982/6988** fax: 04-443 6993
10km (6 miles) from Marrakech. Due to open in 2002, this 'ethnic-chic' riverside complex is earth-built in the traditional style, in a small Berber village. All 14 rooms are suites, with all the trappings of luxury living. Moderate-expensive.

Hidden Palaces

Until 1997 few tourists realised the immense architectural wealth hidden behind the faceless walls of the medina. Most of the *riads* (inward-looking courtyard houses) are havens from the surrounding bustle, protected by thick walls with no outside windows. Their open courtyards, with a cooling fountain and shady fruit trees, are often sumptuously decorated with *zellij* (mosaic), and *zeb* (ornately carved stucco). The ground floor is surrounded by living rooms, finished with elegant *tadlakt* (lime plaster, waxed and polished with agate to the sheen of marble) and *zouak* (painted wood), with bedrooms above and a sun terrace on the roof.

Since the first two 'old house' hotels – **La Maison Arabe** and **Villa des Orangers** – opened their doors, the Europeans have begun quietly to recolonise Marrakech – and this time they have been welcomed with open arms. Over 300 *riads* have now been restored and converted into *maisons d'hôtes* (bed and breakfast), ranging from the simple and charming to the ostentatiously luxurious. Others are available for hire as a whole house, and more are being opened every day (*see* p.88).

Most Marrakchi see the invasion as something entirely positive, injecting new life, jobs and a great many high-spending tourists into the decaying core of the city. The owners of the crumbling and often derelict houses are only too happy to sell – it is their chance to escape to modern blocks with good plumbing and electricity. In 2000 alone, over 1 500 of the old houses were sold in an orgy of restoration. With only 3 000

Tradition and comfort at the Riad Enija, Marrakech.

suitable properties available, prices have already doubled and people are now beginning to talk about shortages. The handful of Moroccans involved are pragmatically funding their own investments by acting as estate agents, while city officials desperately try to catch up with events, ensure proper planning and design and create a system for licensing the *maisons d'hôtes*. In a few short years, these newly magnificent properties have become the single biggest tourist attraction in Marrakech.

Palmeraie Golf Palace *Les Jardins de la Palmeraie, Circuit de Palmeraie, BP 1488* ☎ **04-430 1010**
fax: 04-430 5050
web: www.open.net.ma
Vast, 5-star de luxe holiday resort, in the Palmeraie, about 10 mins drive from the city walls. Five pools, 15 restaurants and bars (including a night-club and karaoke), health and beauty centres, shops and a wide array of sports, including an 18-hole golf course (Robert Trent Jones Snr). Very expensive.
Les Deux Tours *Douar Abiad, Palmeraie, BP 512*
☎ **04-432 9525/6/7**

Les Deux Tours hotel conservatory.

fax: 04-432 9523
Ten kilometres (6 miles) from the centre of Marrakech. Fifteen rooms and ten suites in six luxurious villas, each with its own pool and walled garden. Designed by Charles Boccara, with Turkish and Egyptian influences, along with Moroccan *zellij* (mosaic), *tadlakt* (a cool marble-like surface) and Tataoui (oleander wood). Very expensive.
Hotel Tikida Garden *Circuit de la Palmeraie, BP 1585*
☎ **04-432 9595** fax: 04-432 9599
web: www.marrakech-tikida.com
In the Palmeraie. A comfortable 4-star hotel, with three restaurants, a bar and night-club, tennis courts, jogging track, pool, hammam, fitness centre etc. Popular with tour groups. Moderate.

Further Afield

Essaouira
Hotel Riad Al Madina *9 Rue Attarine* ☎ **04-447 5907**
fax: 04-447 6695/5727
Charming little town centre hotel in a converted 18C merchant's house. Inexpensive.
Sofitel Mogador *Av. Med V, Essaouira* ☎ **04-447 9000**
fax: 04-447 9030/04-447 9090
web: www.sofitel.com
Large, 5-star resort hotel, right on the beach, about 1km from the centre of Essaouira. Pool and international restaurant. The real

draw is a thalassotherapy spa (sea water treatment), with all the trimmings. Expensive.

Ryad Mogador *BP 368, Essaouira* ☎ **04-478 3555** fax: 04-478 3556 web: www.net-tensift.com/mogador Modern 4-star resort hotel with 140 rooms laid out around a large pool, with a coffee shop, international and Moroccan restaurants, beauty salon, hammam, gym, tennis etc. Will arrange water sports. About 4km from the centre of Essaouira, and 300m from the beach. Moderate.

Hotel Villa Maroc *10 Rue Abdellah ben Yassine* ☎ **04-447 6147** fax: 04-447 2806 Comfortable 3-star hotel, created out of three 18C townhouses, with flower filled courtyard and décor sufficiently stylish to attract fashion shoots. Book well ahead. Expensive.

La Maison du Sud *29 Av. Sidi Mohammed Ben Abdellah* ☎ **04-447 4141** web: www.essaouiraweb.com/ maisondusud A charming little hotel located in an 18C riad, near the museum. Moderate.

Around Tizi-n-Test
La Roseraie *BP 769, Marrakech 40 000* ☎ **04-448 5693/04-443 9228** fax: 04-443 9130 web: www.cybernet.net.ma/roseraie High up in the Atlas mountains, 60km (37 miles) from Marrakech,

off the Taroudant road, this is a sybaritic, very European country retreat with fabulous views. Pool, walking, riding, spa and restaurant. Expensive.

Le Sanglier Qui Fume *Ourigane, Marrakech 42150* ☎ **04-448 5707/8** fax: 04 448 5709 Just beyond La Roseraie, in Ouirgane village, 61km (38 miles) from Marrakech, this friendly little hotel is a good place for an overnight stay or lunch stop. The 23 rooms currently vary enormously in quality, as they are gradually renovated, so ask to see a selection. The pleasant food is served in an attractive outdoor restaurant in season. Inexpensive.

Ouarzazate area
Meridien Berbère Palace *Quartier Mansour Eddahbi, Ouarzazate* ☎ **04-488 3105/2139/2967** fax: 04-488 3071 web: www.lemeridien-hotels.com The smartest hotel in town (5-star), supposedly built in a traditional style on a high point between the town centre and kasbah. 240 rooms with private terraces and all mod cons, fine 11ha gardens, restaurant (international and Moroccan food), snack bar, piano bar, disco, tennis courts, fitness centre, hammam and large pool. Expensive.

Hotel Ben Moro *On the outskirts of Skoura, a small town 35km (22 miles) east of Ouarzazate in the*

Dadès Valley ☎ 04-485 2116
fax: 04-485 2026
A fascinating 17C mud-built
kasbah, recently refurbished as a
28-room B&B with a restaurant,
roof terrace, and fabulous views
of the High Atlas mountains and
Kasbah Amerhidil. Moderate.

FOOD AND DRINK
Moroccan Food

Moroccan food is delicious.
Unlike most other North African
foods, it is rarely spicy, although
there are occasional mouth-
numbing exceptions. Above all,
the Moroccans have a sweet tooth
and like nothing better than to
garnish even savoury dishes with
honey and fruit.

Snacks suitable for lunch are a
rarity – people tend to eat the
same *tajines* and *couscous* at
lunchtime and in the evening.
Kebabs are a reasonable
alternative.

Soups come in a variety of
flavours but the most famous is
the hearty *harira*, traditionally
eaten at sunset during Ramadan.
It is a whole meal in itself, with
lamb, lentils and chickpeas, and
served with lemon, *beghrir* (small
pastries doused in honey and
butter), *shebbakia* (cakes fried in
oil and covered in honey) and
dates, for the classic sweet and
sour taste.

Pastilla is a rather startling but
surprisingly delicious light flaky
pastry pie, filled with pigeon
(sometimes complete with
bones), almonds and raisins, and
dusted with sugar.

Méchoui is traditionally
prepared during Aïd el-Khebir
(the lamb festival) and is simply
joints of lamb slowly roasted in
underground clay ovens or spit-
roasted for several hours until soft
as butter.

The same word, *tajine*, is used
both for the distinctive conical
earthenware pot and the meat
(beef or lamb), chicken or fish
stews with vegetables, cooked in
it. Classic recipes include lamb
with prunes, chicken with green
olives and preserved lemons.

Couscous (cracked wheat) is
generally cooked in a light meat
or vegetable stock, and served as
a traditional Friday family lunch.

The Moroccans indulge their
sweet tooth with a lavish array of
incredibly delicious and fattening
pastries, such as the famous
marzipan-filled *cornes de gazelles*,
cakes soaked in honey, almond
feqqas, and *ghoriba* with almonds
or sesame.

Moroccan delights – chicken tagine and lamb with couscous

Drinks

Morocco is a Muslim country and relatively few restaurants and cafés serve alcohol. Even fewer *riads* have a liquor licence but most are prepared to turn a blind eye if you bring in your own bottle of **wine**. Morocco is, however, also a wine-producing country, with some very palatable local vintages, grown around Berkane, Meknès and Boulaouâne. Among the often powerful reds, look out for *Guerrouane, Vieux Papes* and *Cabernet Président*; the best labels among the dry whites include *Oustalet* and *Spéciale Coquillages*; the best of the rosés is probably *Gris de Boulaouâne*. There are also local **beers**, of which Flag

Spéciale and Heineken, brewed under license, are the best.

Soft fizzy drinks are easily available but the best choice for thirst-quenching and taste is the ubiquitous fresh orange juice, served all year in vast quantities at ridiculously cheap prices.

Mint tea, nicknamed 'Berber whisky', is as much a cultural institution as a drink, with small glasses seemingly served every time you sit down. You will be offered a glass of the green liquid, heavily sweetened, not just as a form of refreshment but as a gesture of hospitality and with the wish of good luck (green being a fortuitous colour). Small cups of powerful black coffee are a rarer alternative.

ENJOYING YOUR VISIT

Marrakech Restaurants

Marrakech has a wide array of restaurants but it is still almost always necessary to book ahead for the better places. The food is usually excellent and generally safe to eat, although it is worth casting a quick look over the cleanliness of the cheapest restaurants before sitting down.

Really good Moroccan food tends to come in huge quantities, with a high price tag. Most restaurants have magnificent décor, entertainment, hot and cold running waiters and a set meal which can stretch to seven courses. To eat more cheaply, head for Place Jemaa el Fna. Not only are the evening street stalls excellent but there are numerous small café-restaurants in the surrounding side streets.

'International' cuisine is almost always French, Italian or a mixture of the two, although there are a couple of Vietnamese restaurants, and one or two of the hotels (such as the Sheraton) have an excellent buffet. Most of the European restaurants are in the new town and, while they are attractive, they do not live up to the grandeur of the *riad* restaurants. On the other hand, they are also usually cheaper and involve fewer courses.

Prices

Based on a set meal for one (3-7 courses), without alcohol, you can expect to pay:
Inexpensive: up to 140DH
Moderate: 140DH-350DH
Expensive: above 350DH

Recommendations

In the Medina
Place Jemaa el Fna
One of the most interesting, atmospheric and cheapest places to eat is at the mobile restaurants which take over the place each evening. Trawl the stalls, read the menus and inspect the range of food on show; some have a rather eclectic collection of offal, heads, feet and other items best left to the most adventurous stomachs. Most do delicious food, freshly cooked in front of you. Inexpensive.

Café Argana *see* Cafés, below.
Chez Chegrouni *Place Jemaa el Fna (next to Café Montréal)* Basic local restaurant, with attractive tiled walls, formica tables, paper napkins and heaped plates of food. Verandah overlooking the square. Inexpensive.
Dar Fès *8 Rue Boussouni Elgza, Riad Laarouss* ☎ **04-438 2213**. One of the least touristy and most charming of the *riad*-restaurants, with calming blue décor, superb food and live music. Expensive.
Dar Marjana *15 Derb Sidi Ali Tair, Bab Doukkala* ☎ **04-438 5110/ 5773**. One of the grandest and most luxurious of the *riad*-restaurants; the 7-course set feast is a

The choice is tremendous at the outdoor food stalls on Place Jemaa el Fna.

true theatrical production, from the aperitif in the fountain courtyard to the belly dancer afterwards. The food, service and ambience are all wonderful. Reservation essential. Expensive.

Dar Moha *81 Rue Dar el-Pacha* ☎ **04-438 6400**. Excellent Moroccan cuisine, with an added twist of modern European fusion for fun, in a lavishly decorated *riad* owned by an Italian-Moroccan couple. Expensive.

Dar Yacout *79 Rue Sidi Ahmed Soussi* ☎ **04-438 2929/2900**. The oldest and best known of the *riad*-restaurants, offering a 5-course Moroccan feast with entertainment. Wonderful ambience, with décor by Bill Willis; good if some-

times erratic food; live music and a swimming pool. Frequented by tour groups. Expensive.

Ksar Es Saoussan *3 Derb el-Messaoudyenne, Rue des Ksour* ☎ **04-444 0632**. Stylish, French-owned *riad*-restaurant, serving Moroccan food in the fountain courtyard and surrounding salons. Ask for a guided tour of the rest of the property over drinks. Three fine menus to choose from, according to your appetite. Closed Sunday and throughout August. Moderate-expensive.

Le Pavillon *47 Derb Zaouïa, Bab Doukkala* ☎ **04-439 1240**. A *riad*-restaurant with several attractive small dining rooms surrounding an orange-filled courtyard. The excellent food is French (the only French restaurant in the medina); imposing wine list. Closed lunch time and Tuesday. Expensive.

Le Tobsil *22 Derb Abdallah ben Hessaien, Bab Ksour* ☎ **04-444 4052**. Delightfully restored small *riad*-restaurant, run by women, with excellent traditional food, live music, and charming service. Only 12 tables, so booking is essential. Expensive.

In Guéliz

Al Fassia *232 Av. Mohammed V* ☎ **04-443 4060/444 7237**. Excellent restaurant run entirely by women, with wonderful food and an attractive setting. This is one of the few really good Moroccan restaurants where you can eat à la carte and avoid a six-course feast. Book ahead. Expensive.

Catanzaro *11 Rue Tarik Ibn Ziad, Guéliz* ☎ **04-443 3731**. Excellent, popular small Italian restaurant, specialising in wood-fired grills and pizzas, just behind the Marché de Guéliz. Closed Sunday and through August. Inexpensive.

Le Comptoir Marrakech-Paris *Av. Echouada, Hivernage* ☎ **04-443 7702**. The hippest place in town, with dark aubergine décor and cocktail bar to complement the Moroccan cuisine. Expensive.

Dar Mounia *Rue Khlifa-Ottmane, Bab el Yarmouk* ☎ **04-443 1241** Sumptuous historic house just

outside the walls of the medina, built for the son of El Glaoui, serving a copious *dégustation* menu, which works its way through the entire Moroccan culinary repertoire (although you can order individual dishes if you do not feel you can eat your way through the whole thing). Expensive.

Rôtisserie de la Paix *68 Rue de Yougoslavie* ☎ **04-443 3118**. Generous salads and grills in an attractive shady garden. Moderate.

Bagatelle *101 Rue de Yougoslavie* Here you can dine under a flower-covered vault.

Le Jacaranda *32 Blvd Zerktouni, Guéliz* ☎ **04-444 7215**. Charming French bistro, in a small colonial house, just off Place Abdel Moumen ben Ali. The service is friendly, the menu very affordable and the food excellent. A good place for women to eat out at night. Booking recommended. Open daily for lunch and dinner. Moderate.

Le Jardin Des Arts *6-7 Rue Salia el Hamra, Quartier Semlalia* ☎ **04-444 6634**. French-run restaurant (same management as Villa des Orangers), with excellent food and a strong accent on fish. There is an indoor restaurant but better by far to eat in the lush, peaceful garden, cooled by a waterfall. Moderate.

Les Cépages *9 Rue Ibn Zidoun* ☎ **04-443 9426**. Two beautifully

Dine in opulent traditional Moroccan style at the hotel Mamounia.

designed dining rooms and an outdoor terrace. Generally acknowledged to be the finest French food in Marrakech. Closed Monday. Expensive.

Niagara *31-32 Centre Commercial Ennakhil, Route de Targa* ☎ **04-444 9775**. Actually a short distance out of town but said to have the best pizzas in Marrakech and a favourite of local expats. Closed Monday. Moderate.

Villa Rosa *64 Av. Hassan II* ☎ **04-443 0832**. Just behind the main Post Office. Excellent French and Italian food, with a good selection of fish on offer. Attractive dining room, outdoor terrace and a jazz bar. Closed lunch time. Moderate.

Outstanding Hotel Restaurants

Amanjena – European restaurant (trendy, understated elegance, friendly staff).

La Mamounia – Italian (nightclub atmosphere) and Moroccan restaurants (Moroccan design, set meal, three courses).

Both expensive (*see* Hotels, above).

Cafés

Café Argana *Place Jemaa el Fna, Medina*. The smartest of the many terraced cafés surrounding the square. The food (Moroccan and international) and service are fine, the ice-cream a delight on a hot afternoon and the view from the first floor terrace is excellent.

Get there by 5pm or reserve a table to have a place near the railing.

Café de France *Place Jemaa el Fna, Medina*. Another popular spot, with a ground floor café and traditional tea room, and a third-floor café-restaurant, serving pleasant if uninspired food. Excellent view.

Café Glacier *Place Jemaa el Fna, Medina*. The third of the great viewing platforms and easily confused with the many other places sporting a *café glacier* sign; this is the large one on the south side of the square. It has the best view of the lot but has given up doing anything fancier than fizzy drinks (bought as an entrance fee as you go through the turnstile).

Café les Négociants *Place Abdel Moumen ben Ali, Guéliz*. Comfortable, popular café, next to the main tourist office. French-style coffee and croissants alongside the ubiquitous mint tea and orange juice.

Le Mirador *above the Hotel La Renaissance, Place Abdel Moumen ben Ali, Guéliz*. High-level roof terrace with wonderful views across the whole new city. Also one of the few places in Marrakech, outside the tourist hotels, where you can have a beer. Single women can sit here without hassle or comment. Access by lift from the ground floor café; buy a 15DH voucher for your first drink at the bar, to be allowed into the lift.

Pâtisseries and Ice-cream

Amandine *87 Rue Mohammed el-Bequal, Guéliz.* A luscious supply of French and Moroccan pastries, a tea-room and ice-cream.

Olivieri *7-9 Blvd Mansour Eddahbi, Guéliz.* The best ice-cream in Marrakech. Second branch in Centre Kawkab.

Pâtisserie Al Jawda (also known as Pâtisserie Allami) *11 Rue de la Liberté, Guéliz.* Madame Alammi is undisputed pastry queen of Marrakech, producing a luscious range of tiny Moroccan delicacies.

Pâtisserie Hilton *Place Abdel Moumen ben Ali.* No relation to the hotels, but a wide and delicious array of French and Moroccan pastries and savoury snacks.

Pâtisserie des Princes *32 Bab Agnaou, Medina.* Lip-smacking French and Moroccan pâtisserie in a pedestrianised road just off Place Jemaa el Fna.

Further Afield

Essaouira

If you like grilled fish, why not take a seat at the port, along Rue Bab Douana, where the fish of the day, freshly unloaded from the trawler is cooked in front of you.

Café-Restaurant Taros *2 Rue Sqala, Place Moulay-Hassan* ☎ 04-447 6407. Friendly and comfortable bar and restaurant, with wonderful views from the terrace, three dining rooms with different styles of music, a great library of books on Morocco, and fine Moroccan cuisine, much of it fish-based. Cheap.

Dar Loubane *24 Rue du Rif* ☎ 04-447 6296. Charming restaurant in an 18C old town *riad*, serving imaginative Moroccan and French food. Live Gnaoua music some evenings. Moderate.

Le Coquillage *At the entrance of the fishing port* ☎ 04-447 6655. Attractive seafood restaurant with a busy sun terrace overlooking the town and beach. Live Gnaoua music some evenings. Moderate.

Plates in the souks of the medina.

Ouarzazate area
Chez Dimitri *22 Av. Mohammed V*
☎ **04-488 2653**. Colonial style bar-
brasserie, with early photos of
Ouarzazate, military memorabilia
and wooden tables and chairs.
Wide-ranging menu, including
hearty portions of casseroles.
Cheap.

Hotel-Restaurant la Kasbah
Aït Benhaddou ☎ **04-489 0308**.
In a small village about 30km
(19 miles) north of Ouarzazate,
9km (6 miles) off the Marrakech
road. Simple hotel, with a
terraced restaurant overlooking a
magnificent kasbah. Excellent
lunch stop. Inexpensive.

SHOPPING
What to Buy

Antiques
There are still some genuine
antiques to be found but most are
carefully aged reproductions.
Most vendors are honest but be
careful and remember that there
may be customs regulations to be
negotiated in exporting genuine
antiques.

Clothes
Moroccan dress doesn't always
translate well to a western setting
but it is incredibly comfortable to
wear around the house (*see* p.21).

Ceramics
Terracotta ware includes wonderful garden tubs, urns and jars,
most too big, heavy and fragile to
transport. The most popular
souvenirs are the very reasonably
priced brightly decorative earthenware plates and bowls, with
swirling geometric patterns over a
rich coloured glaze.

Food and Spices
Dried fruit and nuts, olives and
olive oil are some of the best buys.
Moroccan pastries keep for up to
10 days if you can find some way
of transporting them safely (take
your own tin).

Herbalist shops offer a wide
range of herbs and spices, for
both culinary and medicinal use,
with an entertaining sales patter
that often involves a free massage.
Favourite buys include saffron,
cinnamon, cumin, turmeric,
paprika, mixed spices for fish or
meat, ambergris, henna and
essential oils. The best place to
buy spices is the spice bazaar in
the Mellah (near Dar Si Saïd
Museum).

Jewellery
There is plenty of jewellery on
offer, although much of it is too
elaborate for western tastes. The
ornate gold pieces, some set with
precious stones, are usually Arab
in origin; the chunky, heavily patterned silver is generally Berber,
used as a bank by village women.

Leather
There is some wonderful leather-

work for sale but, with the exception of the ubiquitous and highly embroidered slippers, prices are not particularly low. Look out for good quality bags, briefcases and jackets (visitors with time can have them custom-made). There are also plenty of patterned poufs and leather furnishings. Follow the production line from the tanneries through to the souks.

Metalwork

Although the articles are usually too heavy to export, the metalworkers' souk produces wonderful wrought-iron furniture, including mosaic-topped tables at very affordable prices. Also look out for the charmingly patterned lanterns (electric and candle) which can be carried home with care.

Minerals and Fossils

Head up into the mountains and there is a stall on every corner, with a wide array of fossils and crystals, some chemically enhanced into lurid colours but many very beautiful and some, such as the great chunks of amethyst, worth collecting.

Woodwork

There is plenty of woodwork on offer everywhere but the centre of production is Essaouira. Look out both for elegantly simple bowls and boxes, from the beautiful wood and roots of the thuja tree, and for intricately inlaid

Colourful carpets at the Berber auctions in the medina.

marquetry, using lemon wood, ebony, mother of pearl and silver.

Where to Shop

The most entertaining place to shop is in the souk but this can be exhausting and it is probably worth doing some homework in fixed-price shops first.

Ensemble Artisanal
Av. Mohammed V ☎ **04-442 3836**. Just outside the walls, near the Koutoubia. This is a government-run shopping mall of craft shops, offering high quality goods at reasonable fixed prices. It is a good place for noting prices, even if you fancy haggling.

Antiques and Fine Crafts

Dune Galerie *16 Rue la Bahia, Riad Ezitoune El Jdid, Medina* ☎ **04-438 3831**. Fabulous treasure-house of carpets and fine antiques, near the Bahia Palace.
Galerie d'Art Khalid *Dar el Pacha*. Fine selection of antiques and good modern crafts, and Moroccan textiles. Honest dealing.
Galleria Ministero del Gusto *22 Derb Azouz el Moussine* ☎ **04-442 6455**. Exclusive design shop in the souks, filled with splendid furniture and crafts, owned by an Italian woman married to a Moroccan.
Galerie Mourjana *Mouassine Fhal Chiadmi 33/2* ☎ **04-444 2934**. Wonderful Aladdin's cave in the souks.

L'Orientaliste *15 Rue de la Liberté, Guéliz* ☎ **04-443 4074**. French-owned gallery selling antiques, fine crafts, pictures and perfumes.

Books

ACR Librairie d'Art *55 Blvd Zerktouni, Résidence Tayeb, Guéliz* ☎ **04-444 6792**. Small shop near the tourist office with a wonderful collection of books on Morocco and Arabic art, many in English.
Chatr *19-21 Av. Mohammed V, Guéliz* ☎ **04-444 7997/8901**. Good bookshop just north of the tourist office, with a small selection of English novels and a good selection of books on Morocco.

Clothes and Leather

Boutique du Kaftan
38 Av. Mohammed V (next to Regent Restaurant), Guéliz ☎ **04-444 9841**. It doesn't look much at first sight, but this is where the rich and famous of Marrakech come to buy their kaftans.
Place Vendôme *141 Av. Mohammed V* ☎ **04-443 5263**. Long-established and high quality leather shop, off the shelf or custom-made.

There are some very elegant designer boutiques in the shopping mall of **La Mamounia** (for the rich and terminally thin).

Film

Wrédé *142 Av. Mohammed V (near the tourist office)* ☎ **04-443 5739**. The best supply of film and photographic supplies in the city, 1hr developing (prints only) and an optician.

Supermarket

Marjane *Route de Casablanca.* Marrakech's first and only super-market, opened to much excitement in 2000; owned by the French supermarket giant, Carrefour. An excellent place to find essentials (except Marmite), from baby food upwards.

ENTERTAINMENT AND NIGHTLIFE

Bars

There are some bars, but in general they are hard to find and filled with aggressive groups of Moroccan men intent on hard drinking. Definitely not for women but not much fun for men either. The big tourist hotels all have a selection of bars. Dig deep into your pocket and head for one of them. Best and most expensive of all the city centre hotels is La Mamounia, where a drink on the terrace will also buy you access to the finest gardens in Marrakech.

For cheaper, acceptable options, look at a few rooftop terraces:

Hôtel de Foucauld *Rue el Mouahi-dine, Medina.*
Hôtel Tazi *Rue Bab Agnaou* and *Av. Homman el Fetouaki, Medina.*
Le Mirador *above La Renaissance, Place Abdel Moumen ben Ali, Guéliz.*

Casinos

La Mamounia *Hôtel La Mamounia, Av. Bab Jdid* ☎ 04-444 8981. The poshest option in town, with roulette, craps and blackjack and a small selection of machines.
Hotel Es Saâdi *Av. El-Quadissia, Hivernage* ☎ 04-444 8811. Smaller, less glamorous option.

Entrance is free at both. There is no need for a dinner jacket but men should wear a jacket and tie; no jeans or trainers. Take some ID, just in case.

Clubs

There is a selection of clubs and discos, most of them in the tourist hotels. Men should be careful about approaching Moroccan women. If they are 'good' girls, you may get them into serious trouble; if not, they may be one of the many prostitutes who solicit

Typical tourist entertainment.

in the clubs.

Cotton Club *Hôtel Tropicana, Semlalia* ☎ **04-444 7450**.
Diamant Noir *Hôtel Marrakech, Place de la Liberté, Av. Mohammed V* ☎ **04-443 4351**.
New Feeling *Palmeraie Golf Palace* ☎ **04-430 1010**.

Western and Arabic music

Paradise *Mansour Eddahbi Hotel, Av. de France* ☎ **04-444 8222**.

Fantasia

A peculiarly Moroccan and very spectacular form of entertainment, the Fantasia began life as a show of military prowess and involves men on horses galloping around and waving weapons. The tourist version tends to be a full-on Moroccan experience, with added henna artists, musicians, dancers and a feast (expensive).

For details contact **Chez Ali** *Route de Casablanca* ☎ **04-430 7730/444 8187**.

ACTIVITIES
Hot-air balloon/helicopter tours

It is possible to take early morning hot-air balloon trips and helicopter tours, either just around the city, for an aerial view, or a longer journey across the mountains to Ouarzazate and back. Contact: **Ciel d'Afrique** *405 Assif B, 40 000 Marrakech* ☎ **04-430 3135**; fax: 04-430 3196, who offer combined hot air balloon and 4×4 safaris from the Palmeraie.

Calèche rides

If you want to explore Marrakech itself, a charming leisurely way to spend the afternoon is a ride in a **calèche** (horse-drawn carriage) around the walls of the medina, to the Palmeraie or Ménara Gardens. You will find calèches all over the old city but if you have difficulty, try the garden square between Place Jemaa el Fna and the city walls. Base the price on 60-70DH an hour for a carriage seating five (120-150DH for a circuit of the walls).

Fantasia show horsemen.

Cycling

For the more energetic, and temperature permitting, Marrakech is a wonderful place to cycle, although you do need to watch out for traffic, carts, dogs, donkeys and children. There are plenty of places to hire a bike, with prices ranging from about 80-200DII a day. The following do both bikes and mopeds:

Hassan Location *51 Rue de la Recette, Medina* ☎ **04-444 2493**.
Marrakech Motos *31 Route de Casablanca* ☎ **04-444 8359**.

There are also small cycle hire shops in Place 16 Novembre, Guéliz, and on Derb Alsat Moussa, just off Place Jemaa el Fna.

Camel safaris

There are various options for exploring beyond the city, depending on taste and your liking for speed. A slow, but by no means smooth, option is to try a camel safari. There are several places in and around Marrakech where you can have a quick 10-minute ride and photo opportunity on a camel. For those masochists who want more, several operators run 2-3 day camel safaris into the desert from Ouarzazate.

Quad bikes

These provide a really satisfying way to get thoroughly dusty, rambling through the local countryside. Contact **Locaquad** *Palmavira, 8km (5 miles) along Route de Fès* ☎ **04-430 5854**.

Sightseeing excursions

For sightseeing excursions it is easy to hire a car and do self-drive trips to the Berber markets and the surrounding countryside but consider taking a guided tour of the Berber villages. You will gain access to the villages that you would not get on your own and will learn a great deal more about the local lifestyle. Ask for details at your hotel, the tourist office or any local travel agent.

Jeep safaris

A four-wheel drive is often the only way to get into the more remote areas of the High Atlas, whether your interest is in Berbers, birds, botany or the jeep itself. Most hotels, travel agents and the tourist office will organise guided jeep safaris. It is recommended that you take a guide, owing to the distinct lack of good maps in the mountains. You can also hire your own vehicle (*see* Car Hire, p. 112).

Hammam

After all that activity, dust and exhilaration, what better way to relax than in a hammam? The hammam, descended from the Roman bath, is a delightful and absurdly cheap way to unwind. The full treatment involves having your skin oiled and scraped, a massage, steam room and cold shower, followed by lounging around being sociable. There are always separate sections for men and women. The locals will be happy to show you the ropes.

Many of the larger hotels and some of the *riads* have their own, otherwise ask where you can find one locally – they are rarely obvious from the outside. Contact:

Hammam Dar el-Bacha *20 Rue Fatima Zohra, Medina*, near Club Méditerranée, behind Place Jemaa el Fna.

Hammam Safi *Blvd de Safi, Guéliz*, near the Majorelle Garden.

SPORTS

The Country Club *Les Jardins de la Palmeraie, Palmeraie Golf Palace* ☎ 04-430 2045/1010 is the best all-round sporting venue in the city and a wonderfully sybaritic escape from the heat and hassle of the medina. The 100DH entry

fee gives you access, sunbathing and swimming. Drinks, food, tennis, golf and horse-riding cost extra.

Golf

There are three excellent 18-hole golf courses in the Palmeraie Country Club, near Marrakech, and one in Ouarzazate:

Golf de la Palmeraie (see above)
Royal Golf de Marrakech ☎ 04-440 4705/444 4341.
Golf d'Amelkis ☎ 04-440 3046/4414.
Royal Golf de Ouarzazate ☎ 04-488 2218/488 2486.

Swimming

Most of the large hotels have good pools and even a few of the *riads* have plunge pools for cooling off. Otherwise head for the Palmeraie Country Club (see above) or the Sheraton (80DH a day).

Riding

It is possible to ride just out of town or do more challenging rides in the High Atlas (see also Specialist Tour Operators below):

Centre Équestre La Roseraie *BP 10, Asni-Marrakesh* ☎ 04-443 2094.
Ranch de la Palmeraie *Circuit de la Palmeraie* ☎ 04-431 3130.

Tennis

Many of the larger hotels also have tennis courts. Alternatives are the Palmeraie Country Club or **Tennis Club** *Rue Oued el-Makhazine, Quartier de l'Hivernage* ☎ 04-443 1902.

Skiing
In theory it is possible to ski in Oukaïmeden (*see* p.73) in winter but the quality and quantity of snow varies enormously from year to year (see Specialist Tour Operators, below). For information, contact the **Royal Moroccan Ski and Mountain Federation** *Parc de la Ligue Arabe, Casablanca* ☎ 02-220 3798; web site: www.skiin.com/static/resorts/resort.pl/oukaim-main2.en.html

Specialist Tour Operators
Adrar Aventures *111 Quartier Essaada* ☎ 04-443 9388. Hiking, trekking, riding, skiing.

Algeria-Tours *Villa Ourida, Quartier Saadia* ☎ 04-443 4793. Hiking, trekking, skiing.

Atlas Sahara Trek *6 bis, Rue Houdhoud, Quartier Majorelle* ☎ 04-431 3901. Hiking, trekking, riding, fishing, whitewater rafting, skiing.

Loisirs et Voyages *37 Blvd El Mansour Eddahbi* ☎ 04-443 5041. Hiking and trekking.

Sport Travel *154 Av. Mohammed V* ☎ 04-443 9968. Hiking, trekking, riding, whitewater sports, skiing.

Tourisport *213 Av. Mohammed V* ☎ 04-444 8165. Hiking, trekking, riding, skiing, whitewater sports.

Voyage Voyages *194/7 Résidence Firdaous, Rue Mohammed el-Baqual 15, Guéliz* ☎ 04-442 0667; fax: 04-443 0310. Sightseeing, 4×4 safaris, trekking, riding, skiing, golf, hunting, fishing.

Setting off on the great adventure.

THE BASICS

Before You Go

All visitors need a valid passport. Nationals of the EU, Australia, Canada, New Zealand, South Africa and the USA will receive a free 90-day tourist visa on arrival. There are no mandatory inoculations. It is, however, sensible to be vaccinated against tetanus, polio, typhoid and hepatitis A and B. Travel insurance with full medical cover is strongly recommended.

Getting There

By Air

Royal Air Maroc has three flights a week from London Stansted to Marrakech, **GB Airways** operates five flights a week from Heathrow (touching down in Casablanca) under the BA banner, and there are some direct charter flights from the UK. Other flights are all via Casablanca. With the boom in tourism, flights are in short supply, so book ahead and remember to confirm 72 hours before departure.

Marrakech-Ménara International Airport
☎ 04-444 7910/7865/8506
fax: 04-444 9219
web: www.onda.org.ma/
aeroport/marrakch
5km (3 miles) southwest of the city centre. In theory, bus no 11

leaves for Place Jemaa el Fna every 30 minutes, but the easiest way into the city centre is by *petit taxi*.

Airline addresses in Marrakech
Air France
197 Av. Mohammed V, Guéliz
☎ 04-444 6444/04-443 6205
fax: 04-444 6002
web: www.airfrance.com
GB Airways Ménara Airport
☎ 04-444 8951
web: www.britishairways.com
Royal Air Maroc
197 Av. Mohammed V, Guéliz
☎ 04-443 6205 fax: 04-444 6002
National call centre
☎ 0900-00 800
web: www.royalairmaroc.com

By Train

The railway station is situated off Av. Hassan II (☎ 04-444 7947), on the edge of Guéliz, about 1.5km (1 mile) west of the post office. The national railway is **ONCF** (☎ 07-777 6520 web: www.oncf.org.ma/voyageurs). Marrakesh has a station but few trains – four a day from Casablanca and one from Fès. Under-26 Inter-rail cards are valid in Morocco.

By Coach

The coach station is at Place el-Mouarabitène, just outside Bab Doukkala, on the northwestern edge of the old city (☎ 04-443 3933). There are frequent long-distance coaches to all other major cities and smaller regional towns. The best and largest of the Moroccan operators is **CTM** (☎ **04-443 4651** web: www.ctm. co.ma). Book at least a day ahead and always double-check the timetable.

By Car

To take your own vehicle into the country, you need full insurance and a Green Card. For a caravan, trailer or motor boat, you also need a customs certificate or triptych, and it is sensible to obtain an international camping and caravanning passbook. Cars, caravans and mobile homes are not allowed to stay in Morocco more than six months. You may drive on your national driving licence. The minimum age for driving is 21 years.

Driving to Marrakech, which is some distance from the coast, involves quite a journey. Most arrive at Tangier, in the north, after driving through Spain and sailing from Algeciras, or from the south of France at Sète.

Brush shoulders with the locals in Marrakech's bustling souks.

Accommodation see **p.84**

Airports see **Getting There, p.110**

Bicycles see **p.106**

Books

The Traveller's History of North Africa, Barnaby Rogerson (Windrush Press)

Culture Shock! Morocco, Orin Hargreaves (Kuperard)

Moroccan Cuisine, Paula Wolfert (Grub Street)

Cooking at the Kasbah, Kitty Morse (Chronicle)

Zillij: The Art of Moroccan Ceramics, Salma Damluji (Garnet)

Majorelle: a Moroccan Oasis, Madison Cox *et al* (Thames & Hudson)

Travelogue and fiction:

The Voices of Marrakesh, Elias Canetti (M Boyars)

Lords of the Atlas, Gavin Maxwell (Cassell)

A Year in Marrakech, Peter Mayne (Eland Books)

Their Heads are Green, and *Points in Time*, Paul Bowles

(Peter Owen)

Hideous Kinky, Esther Freud (Penguin)

Morocco, The Traveller's Companion, Margaret and Robin Bidwell (IB Taurus) – an anthology of travel writing

Buses see **p.126**

Camping

There are three campsites in Marrakech (one in Guéliz, the others a few kilometres out of town) but the standard is not high and it would be better to stay in a cheap hotel.

Car Hire

You have a choice between all the main international companies and many local ones. Prices start at about 400DH a day, all-inclusive for a small car, 1300DH a day for a 4×4, self-drive. Remember that a small car may have trouble on the steep mountain roads. A car with a driver can actually be cheaper, thanks to lower insurance premiums.

Always, Complex Kawkab, Guéliz

☎ 04-444 6797; fax: 04-443 0938
Avis, 137 Av. Mohammed V
☎ 04-443 3727; web: www.avis.
com; Airport office: ☎ 04-443 31
69
Budget, Blvd Zerktouni, Guéliz
☎ 04-443 1180; web: www.
budgetrentacar.com; also offices
at the airport (☎ 04-483 8875)
and La Mamounia (☎ 04-444
0720)
Concorde Cars, 154 Av.
Mohammed V ☎ 04-443 9973
Europcar, 63 Blvd Zerktouni,
Guéliz ☎ 04-443 1228; fax: 04-
443 2769; web: www.europcar.
com
Hertz, 154 Av. Mohammed V,
Guéliz ☎ 04-443 9984; fax: 04-
443 9989; web: www.hertz.com;
Airport office ☎ 04-444 7230
Nomade Car, 112 Av.
Mohammed V, Guéliz (next to
Les Négociants) ☎ 04-444 7126;
fax: 04-443 5286
Novaloc, 61 Rue de Yougoslavie,
passage Ghandori, Guéliz ☎ 04-
443 2493/3961; fax: 04-440 9587
Voyage Voyages, 194/7
Résidence Firdaous, Rue
Mohammed el Baqal 15, Guéliz
☎ 04-442 0667; fax: 04-443 0310

Children

The Moroccans love children
and go out of their way to make
them welcome. The streets are
safe, the food is good and
hygienic, and there are plenty of
simple options which children
will eat.

Supplies for small babies are
easily available at the French-
owned supermarket (Marjane,
Route de Casablanca) and there
are good pharmacies and
doctors. It is probably best to
avoid high summer, when the
heat will be overwhelming, and
you may have to cope with a
minor dose of diarrhoea as their
stomachs adjust but there should
be no more sinister complica-
tions.

There are no specific attrac-
tions for children but they will
love the colourful streetlife and
a trip to the mountains or
seaside will give them space to
rampage.

Churches see Religion

Climate see p.83

Clothing

You don't need to take the veil
but do dress moderately
respectably – mini-skirts, shorts
and skimpy tops should be kept
for the hotel grounds and
swimming pool. In summer the
weather is extremely hot, so take
loose, natural fibres. In winter, it
can be surprisingly cold, in spite
of the sunny days, and you will
need something reasonably
warm for the evenings right
through until April. Dress in the
evenings is usually smart-casual.

Clothing sizes in Morocco are
the same as in Europe:

Women's sizes

UK	8	10	12	14	16	18
Europe	38	40	42	44	46	48
US	6	8	10	12	14	16

Women's shoes

UK	4.5	5	5.5	6	6.5	7
Europe	38	38	39	39	40	41
US	6	6.5	7	7.5	8	8.5

Men's suits

UK/US	36	38	40	42	44	46
Europe	46	48	50	52	54	56

Men's shirts

UK/US	14	14.5	15	15.5	16	16.5	17
Europe	36	37	38	39/40	41	42	43

Men's shoes

UK	7	7.5	8.5	9.5	10.5	11
Europe	41	42	43	44	45	46
US	8	8.5	9.5	10.5	11.5	12

Crime

Crime is relatively low, but it does exist and sensible precautions should be taken against the risk of petty theft. Take care of wallets and bags in Place Jemaa el Fna and the souks, particularly in the evenings. Women are safe walking around the medina at any time of day but should be more cautious in the new town at night.

• Carry as little money and as few credit cards as possible and leave any valuables in the hotel safe.

• Carry wallets and purses in secure pockets and carry handbags across your body or firmly under your arm.

• Cars are often targeted so never leave your car unlocked and hide away or, better still, remove items of value.

• Beware of drug trafficking; never accept or agree to carry packages from strangers nor leave bags unattended, particularly at airports.

Currency see Money

Customs and Entry Regulations

The following allowances apply per adult when entering Morocco: 1 bottle of wine and 1 bottle of spirits, or 3 bottles of wine; 200 cigarettes, or 50 cigars, or 250g of tobacco.

There is no problem taking in a camera or video-recorder but professional photographic equipment has to be declared and licensed. It is forbidden to import or export *dirhams*.

When returning home (all EU countries), the following guidelines for duty-free or goods bought outside the EU apply: 200 cigarettes, or 100 cigarillos, or 50 cigars, or 250g tobacco; 1 litre of spirits, or 2 litres of sparkling or fortified wine and 2 litres of still wine; 50g perfume or 250cc of toilet water.

Disabled Visitors

Marrakech is very flat but facilities are generally poor everywhere. Getting around the medina, with its cobbled streets, stepped alleys and narrow passages, will be very difficult. On the other hand, some of the larger hotels have properly designed rooms, the people are kind, generous and willing to help, and with some effort it should be possible to get to many places. Don't be put off trying but plan ahead very carefully.

For information before you travel contact:

UK
RADAR (Royal Association for Disability and Rehabilitation), 12 City Forum, 250 City Road, London EC1V 8AF ☎ **020 7250 3222**; fax: 020 7250 1212.
Holiday Care Service, 2nd Floor, Imperial Buildings, Victoria Rd, Horley, Surrey RH6 7PZ ☎ **01293 774 535**.

USA
SATH (Society for the Advancement of Travel for the Handicapped), 347 Fifth Ave, Suite 610, New York, NY10016 ☎ **212 447 7284**; fax: 212 725 8253.
Mobility International USA, PO Box 10767, Eugene, Oregon 97440 ☎ **541 343 1284**.

Driving
Out of town, Morocco has excellent roads and there are fast connections to Casablanca and Essaouira. The roads across the mountains to Ouarzazate and Taroudant are difficult, with

hairpin bends, long drops and few crash barriers. Always watch out for small children and goats.

A car is a severe hindrance within the old city; if you have one, park it or leave it at your hotel, and walk or use taxis. The new town has good, wide roads and driving is easy.
Car parks: There is very limited on-street parking in the old town but there are car parks in Place Jemaa el Fna (in front of Hotel Foucauld and behind the CTM Hotel) and behind the Koutoubia. All the larger hotels in Guéliz have some parking for guests. You can park anywhere in the new town not marked by red and white stripes on the

Musician in Place Jemaa el Fna.

pavement. An unofficial parking attendant will probably pop up and offer to watch your car. Tip a couple of *dirhams* on your return.

Rules: Drive on the right. Seat belts are compulsory. Speed limits are: 40kph/25mph in town; 100kph/62mph on open roads. There are frequent road-blocks outside town, so keep your papers handy. On-the-spot fines are rarely high, so pay up but ask for a receipt. Drivers are not permitted to drink any alcohol.

Fuel: Petrol is only fractionally cheaper than in the UK. There are plenty of petrol stations in Guéliz and on the main roads out of Marrakech, but if you are travelling out of the city you would be wise to fill up first. Not all garages take credit cards.

For further information contact: **Touring Club du Maroc** ☎ **04-427 9288**.

Emergency breakdown service is provided by AXA Insurance Company ☎ **02-267 272**, with nationwide breakdown cover for foreign motorists.

See also **Before You Go, Car Hire**

Dry-Cleaning *see* Laundry

Electric Current

The current is 220V AC, 50 cycles in all newer buildings; some older ones are still 110V. Most plugs are the round, two-pin variety so you will need an adaptor if you are taking your own appliances.

Embassies and Consulates

Embassies and consulates can be found at the following addresses:
Australia: contact UK embassy
Canada: 13 Bis, Rue Jaafar Assadik, Agdal, BP 709, Rabat ☎ **212-367 2880**; fax: 212-367 2178
Ireland: contact UK embassy
New Zealand: contact UK embassy
UK: 17 Blvd de la Tour Hassan, BP 45, Rabat ☎ **212-7-72 09 05/06/73; 1403/04/70 4532**; fax: 212-7-70 4531
USA: 13 Av. Ahmed Balafrej, Rabat ☎ **212-7-75 81 81/76 22 65**; fax: 212-7-75 08 63

Emergencies

Police: ☎ **19**
Tourist police: ☎ **04-438 4601**
Fire/ambulance: ☎ **15**
SOS Médecins: ☎ **04-440 4040**
Car breakdown: ☎ **177**
Information: ☎ **016**

Etiquette

Moroccans are immensely hospitable people. If invited into someone's home, take a small gift for the children (sweets or pastries). Always wash your hands before a meal, which will probably begin with grace ('Bismillah' – in praise of God). Use only your right hand to eat.

Taste everything but you are not expected to eat everything put in front of you. Mint tea is offered as a sign of hospitality and should be accepted; expect your glass to be refilled up to three times.

Don't drink, eat or smoke in public during daylight hours in Ramadan, a time of fasting for all Muslims. Non Muslims are not allowed into any mosques. It is not necessary to cover up too much but anyone wearing skimpy miniskirts, shorts or very revealing tops may expect some disapproval from more traditional people and too much interest from younger men.

Haggling is a way of life that extends from the bazaar to the boardroom. Negotiations are generally informal and cheerful events.

Health

There are few serious health risks in Marrakech. It is probably sensible to keep up the main inoculations (*see* **Before You Go**) and drink bottled water (this should also be used for cleaning your teeth). The food is usually safe, even in Place Jemaa el Fna, but avoid salad that has been sitting around uncovered for any length of time and make sure that meat has been freshly cooked. In summer, use a hat and sunblock and drink plenty throughout the day. Use prophy-

lactics if required – there is AIDS here, as everywhere else.

You may fall foul of various biting and stinging insects but there is no malaria in Morocco and a simple sting relief should be sufficient. If you have any sort of reaction, consult a pharmacist. There are snakes and scorpions in the countryside so watch where you climb on the rocks.

Pharmacies: Moroccan pharmacies are able to deal with a wide range of minor ailments and even prescribe antibiotics over the counter. Try Pharmacie de Paris, Av. Mohammed V ☎ 04-444 7663 (next to Café les Negociants), where the excellent pharmacist, Mohammed

Anyone for fresh orange juice?

Abouyoub, speaks English; or
Pharmacies de Garde, Place
Jemaa el Fna ☎ 04-443 0415 and
Rue Khalid Ben Oualid ☎ 04-
443 0415 (24hr opening).
Doctors and dentists: Most hotels
will be able to find you an
English-speaking doctor or
dentist. Many of them trained in
France and the standard of care
is generally good. Dr Reitzer,
Rue de la Liberté ☎ 061-17 38
03, is a good French doctor who
speaks excellent English.
Hospital: There are no recipro-
cal agreements for medical cover
so travel insurance is essential.
The hospitals generally lack
resources; the best, by some way,
is the private Polyclinique du
Sud, 2 Rue de Yougoslavie,
Guéliz ☎ 04-444 7999/443 7999;
freephone: ☎ 0800 2525.

In case of serious problems,
try to go home.

Language

The majority of people speak
Moroccan Arabic as their first
language (the written form is
always classical Arabic).
Relatively few townspeople speak
one of the Berber languages
common to the surrounding
mountains. Most people speak at
least some words of French and a
sufficient number speak it well
enough for you to get by without
ever having to learn Arabic. A
few words and phrases are given
on the page opposite.

Laundry

Most hotels offer a laundry
service. There are also commercial laundries and dry-cleaners,
which are reasonably priced, but
can be heavy on the clothes.

Lost Property

There is no central lost property
office. You could try the tourism
police but, if you've lost something, it has probably gone for
ever.

Maps and Guides

The Michelin **sheet map 959** will
enable you to plan your routes if
touring Morocco or planning
excursions from Marrakech. The
Michelin Green Guide Maroc
(French edition only) contains
information on Marrakech,
including street maps, together
with details of sights and attrac-
tions you may wish to visit on any
day trips or excursions.

Media

There are no local English
language publications.
Moroccan French newspapers
include the royalist *Le Matin du
Sahara*, Istiqlal Party *L'Opinion*
and socialist *Libération*. It is
possible to obtain foreign
language papers a day late. Look
at the kiosk near the tourist
office on Place Abdel Moumen
ben Ali or try the shop in front
of La Mamounia hotel.

Local TV stations broadcast in

English	French	Arabic
Welcome	Bienvenue	Ya marhaba
Hello (informal)	Salut	Labes
Good morning/ afternoon	Bonjour	Essalam/ Salam alaykoum
Good evening	Bonsoir	Msa el-khir
Good night	Bonne nuit	Leela saïda
Goodbye	Au revoir	Bislemah
Yes	Oui	Nam
No	Non	Lalal
Please	S'il vous plaît	Men fadlak
Thank you	Merci	Choukrane
Excuse me	Pardon	Afouan
OK	D'accord	Wakha
No problem	Pas de problème	Meckee mushkeel
Sir/Madam	Monsieur/Madame	Si, Sidi/Lalla
I don't understand	Je ne comprends pas	Ma fhemchi
I don't know	Je ne sais pas	Ma arafshi
Help!	Au secours!	Ateqq!
WC/bathroom	Toilettes	Vaysay
Beware	Attention!	Roud balek
Where is …?	Où est …?	Feen kayn …?
When is …?	Quand est …?	Waqtash …?
How much is this?	Combien coûte ceci?	Chhal hadi?
Write it	Écrivez-le	Ktib ha
Too expensive	Trop cher	Ghalee bzef
1	Un	Whad
2	Deux	Jouj
3	Trois	Tlata
4	Quatre	Reba
5	Cinq	Khemsa
6	Six	Setta
7	Sept	Seba
8	Huit	Tmenya
9	Neuf	Tasoud
10	Dix	Achra
100	Cent	Mia
1000	Mille	Alef

both French and Arabic but the quality is less than riveting. Many hotels have French and Italian satellite channels but you will be very lucky to find English language channels, even BBC or CNN.

There are plenty of local radio stations playing Arabic music. It is possible to pick up BBC World Service (9.41 and 5.975 mhz/ 31.88 and 50.21m).

Money

The Moroccan *dirham* is one of the more stable currencies in North Africa, chiefly because it cannot be traded freely and is kept artificially high by the Moroccan authorities. You are not allowed to import or export *dirham*; if you cannot change any money on arrival, many people are happy to accept French francs, although the price will probably be higher. Keep hold of exchange receipts if you want to convert your remaining *dirham* on departure.

Notes come in denominations of 10, 20, 50, 100 and 200DH. Coins come in denominations of 1, 5 and 10DH, and 5, 10, 20 and 50 centimes. Try and keep a plentiful supply of small change for taxis, tips etc.

Major credit cards are widely accepted in the official shops, and larger hotels and restaurants, although there are some surprising exceptions. The souks mainly operate a cash economy but are quite happy to deal in any hard currency.

There are exchange facilities and ATMs which will accept foreign cards at some (but not all) banks. You will usually fare better in the new town (along Av. Mohammed V) than in the area around Place Jemaa el Fna, if you want to find a working ATM.

In emergencies, use Western Union to transfer money via **Wafabank**, 212 Av. Mohammed V; ☎ 04-443 6588, or **Barid al Maghrib**, Place du 16 Novembre ☎ 04-443 1953, both in Guéliz.

Opening Hours

Banks: Mon-Thur 8.15/30-11.30am/noon, 2.15/30-4pm, Fri 8.15/30-11.15am, 2.45-4pm.
Post Offices: Mon-Fri, 8.30am-6.30pm, Sat 8.30am-12.30pm.
Shops: Usually open Mon-Sat 9am-8/9pm, some closing for lunch. Some, including those in the souks, remain open on Sunday.
Museums and sights: Usually open Tues-Sun 9am-noon, 3-5pm.
Tourist Office: Mon-Fri, 8.30am-noon, 3.30-6.30pm.

Photography

A good range of print film and a narrower range of slide film is available in Marrakech, and is significantly cheaper than in the UK. It is also easy to get prints developed, although slides have to go to Casablanca and take three days.

Selecting a film is difficult. The midday light is very harsh but the narrow alleys create deep shadows. It is illegal to photograph any military installation and inside some museums. Museums that do allow photography may forbid the use of flash.

While everyone is happy for you to photograph the architecture, expect to pay a hefty tip (about 5DH) to photograph people. Ask before shooting and be prepared to take no for an answer, particularly among women.

Police

Police emergency: ☎ 19
Tourist police: Place Jemaa el Fna ☎ 04-438 4601

There are many sorts of police in Marrakech – dealing with locals, tourists, and traffic, in town and out of town. When in doubt, head for the tourist police, who are schooled in the art of being nice to foreigners, and should be able to find someone who speaks English. Be prepared to get thoroughly entangled in red tape. If anything is stolen, make sure you get a crime report for the insurance company. As ever, it is probably sensible to take a friend as witness to any proceedings and, if in any doubt, phone your embassy.

Post Offices

The main post office is at Place du 16 Novembre, Guéliz ☎ 04-443 0977. Opening hours (*see* p.120). Ask for poste restante at counter no 6. There is also a good post office in Place Jemaa el Fna.

You can buy stamps from many tobacconists (*tabacs*) and from some hotels and tourist shops. *See also* **Opening Hours**

Public Holidays

Morocco operates with two different calendars – the western Gregorian calendar, (which official secular holidays follow) and the Hegira, the Islamic

Delicate plasterwork.

calendar which began on 16 July 622, the day Mohammed left Mecca for Medina (and which religious holidays follow). It is based on the lunar cycle and has 12 months but is shorter than the Gregorian calendar, so the dates of religious festivals vary each year.

Official Holidays

1 Jan – New Year's Day
11 Jan – Independence Day
1 May – Labour Day
23 May – National Day
9 June – Young People's Day
30 July – Throne Day (marking the accession to the throne of Mohammed VI, with fireworks, parades and dancing)
14 Aug – Allegiance of Wadi-Eddahab
20 Aug – Anniversary of the Revolution
6 Nov – Anniversary of the Green March
18 Nov – Return from exile of Mohammed V

Religious Holidays

Ramadan – month-long fast. Muslims do not eat or drink between the hours of sunrise and sunset. Not a good time to visit if you want to get things done but the night-time parties can be good fun.
Aïd el-Fitr – riotous celebration to mark the end of Ramadan
Aïd el-Kebir – Feast of Abraham's sacrifice; people all slaughter and eat lamb
First of Moharam – start of Hegira (Islamic New Year)
Mouloud an-Nabi – birth of the Prophet
Moussems – these are local religious festivals celebrating the lives of a particular saint. The religious pilgrimage to the tomb or shrine is often a colourful occasion, accompanied by fantasias, fairs, music, dance and food. The three most important in Marrakech are in September but there are others in the outlying areas at various times of year. Ask the tourist office if there are any happening while you are there.

Religion

Morocco is a Muslim country and the official religion is Islam. Most people are devout but do not make a huge show of it. The government clamped down hard on the first stirrings of funda-mentalism spreading from Algeria. In Guéliz you will find a Roman Catholic church and a synagogue, and there are still a couple of old synagogues in the Mellah. There are around 300 mosques in the city. Non-Muslims are not allowed to enter any of them.

Smoking

The number of people who smoke is significantly higher than in the UK or USA and there are virtually no areas set aside for non-smokers, even in restaurants. Only a few Moroccan women have started to smoke but mostly in private or in trendy New Town cafés. As smoking is one of the pleasures forgone by Muslims during Ramadan, foreigners should refrain from smoking in public in daylight hours during this period.

Stamps see Post Offices

Telephones

There are plenty of public call boxes which take either coins or credit cards. For long-distance calls it is probably easier to use a *teleboutique*, where you pay at the end of the call; these are liberally scattered across the town.

GSM mobiles work here. If you are in town for any length of time and want to receive a lot of local calls, consider buying a local pay-as-you-go SIM card.

It is possible to send faxes from most hotels and *teleboutiques*.

There are a couple of internet cafés in the medina but there are many more in Guéliz.

Useful codes:
Morocco country code
(from abroad) ☎ 212
Marrakech area code ☎ 04
To direct dial abroad
☎ 00 + country code
Operator ☎ 100
International operator ☎ 120
Local directory enquiries ☎ 160

Time

Morocco time follows Greenwich Mean Time (GMT) all year round. During the summer it is one hour behind the UK and six hours ahead of eastern USA (Eastern Standard Time).

Tipping

It is a good idea to have plenty of small change in your pocket, as guides, waiters, petrol pump and parking attendants expect a tip. Keep the amounts in proportion, even if you are staying in a 5-star hotel. Remember that many families are surviving on less than 500DH a week and an income of US$400 a month is enough to keep people in some style. Also beware of handing out *dirhams* too readily to appealing children, as you will be followed by a clamouring horde; most are happy with a few sweets.

Hotel staff: About 5DH for the porter, doorman or room service. About the same, per day, for the chambermaid.

Restaurants: Service is usually included (although they will often understandably say it is not, if asked directly) but it is customary to leave a few *dirhams*.

Taxis: It is unnecessary to tip, although a couple of *dirhams* for a driver who uses the meter without being asked is a good incentive for the future.

Parking attendants: 2DH an hour for the unofficial guardians who patrol the pavements.

Monuments: A custodian who opens a locked area for you will expect a small gratuity.

Photography: The going rate for a photo is about 5DH, although you'll get asked for more.

Guides: 30DH for a half-day, if they were good.

Also leave a couple of *dirhams* for good barmen, café waiters, toilet attendants, and petrol pump attendants.

Toilets

The museums, sights, stations, cafés and restaurants all have good public toilets. Other than this, they are rare and generally unpleasant. Carry your own supply of tissues. If there is an attendant, tip about 2-3DH.

Tourist Information Offices

You can obtain information before you go from the **Moroccan National Tourist Board (ONMT)**, website: www.tourism-in-morocco.com They have offices in:

Australia: 11 West Street North, Sydney NSW 2060 ☎ 612-922 4999; fax: 612-923 1053

Canada: Place Montréal, 1800 Rue Mac Gill, Suite 2450, Montréal, Canada H3A 3J6 ☎ 514-842 8111/2; fax: 514-842 5316

UK: 205 Regent St, London W1R 7DE ☎ 020-7437 0073; fax: 020-7734 8172

USA: 20 East 46th St, Suite 1201, New York, NY 10017 ☎ 212-557 2520/1/2; fax: 212-949 8148 Lake Buena Vista, PO Box 2263, Orlando, Florida 32830 ☎ 407-827 5337/5; 407-827 5129

The Moroccan National Tourist Board or Syndicat d'Initiative offices in Morocco can supply you with brochures, official guides, maps and information on hotels and local festivals:

Marrakech

Moroccan National Tourist Board, Place Abdel Moumen ben Ali, Av. Mohammed V ☎ 04-443 6239/6179; fax: 04-443 6057. Open Mon-Fri, 8.30am-noon and 3.30-6.30pm. Syndicat d'Initiative (GRIT), 176 Av. Mohammed V ☎ 04-443 0886. Open Mon-Fri, 8.30am-noon and 2.30-6.30pm.

Essaouira

10 Rue du Caire ☎ 04-475 080; fax: 04-783 530; web: www.mogador-essaouira.com

Ouarzazate

Av. Mohammed V ☎ 04-488 24 85; fax: 04-488 52 90

Tours

Tour guides: There are around 300 official tour guides in Marrakech, bookable through the tourist office or most hotels. Working in a variety of languages, they offer half- and full-day walking tours of the medina, taking in all the major sights and the souks. Some are excellent; others have poor language skills and too much interest in taking you to their cousin's shop. Hiring a guide for at least one session is well worth while – it is about the only way to find your way around the impenetrable maze of alleyways. It's the luck of the draw who you get but don't be afraid to ask for a change if you are unhappy. At the time of writing, they cost 250-300DH a day.

Unofficial tour guides: Seemingly hundreds of other people offer their services as unofficial guides. Children are useful for finding a specific address for you (such as the *riad* you lost when you left that morning) but otherwise don't be conned.

Out of town: There is a wide range of out of town excursions on offer (*see* p.109).

Transport

Marrakech looks small – it is possible to walk from one end of the medina to the other in a brisk 30 minutes – but it can be hard on the feet and good shoes are essential. You will be walking a lot, as there are many places where cars cannot go.

Taxis: There are two sorts of taxi. *Petit taxis*, licensed for three passengers and small enough to negotiate many of the narrow streets of the medina, are cheap, easy and ubiquitous. By law, the drivers are meant to use the

Passing by the Royal Palace, Marrakech.

meter and most will do so, if asked, but they prefer to try and negotiate flat fees. At the time of writing, a journey within the medina is almost never more than 12DH, while a trip from the medina to Guéliz is 15-20DH. There are taxi ranks but you can flag down taxis in the street without difficulty. If they already have passengers, they simply deliver them en route.

Grands taxis are larger cars (often Mercedes), usually used as shared taxis, but they are also used for airport runs and longer trips to outlying districts.

Buses: The local buses, designed primarily to bring in workers from outlying suburbs, all converge on Rue Moulay Ismaïl, next to the small garden square between Place Jemaa el Fna and the city walls. Useful buses include no 1 (Av. Mohammed V); no 2 (bus station); no 3 (Av. Mohammed V and the train station); no 11 (airport and Menara Gardens); and no 14 (Av. Mohammed V and the train station).

Useful Websites

Many of the best websites on Morocco are in French. These are a few of the better ones in English:
www.bestofmaroc.com – useful tourism site
www.tourism-in-morocco.com – official tourist office website
www.mincom.gov.ma – government facts and figures
www.mpep.gov.ma – people-based government statistics
www.morocco.com – useful portal with good links
www.maroc.net

Vaccinations see Before You Go, p.110

Water

The tap water is probably clean but it is advisable never to drink (or clean your teeth with) anything other than bottled or boiled water. Avoid ice cubes which may have been made with tap water. There are excellent local bottled mineral waters: Sidi Ali (still) and Sidi Hazarem (fizzy), which are widely available.

Women Travellers

Expect some degree of hassle, whatever your age or looks – Moroccans love to flirt. On the whole, however, it is good-humoured and non-aggressive and you won't be in any danger. If you feel cornered, speak loudly and firmly – the potential for public shame will soon stop the harassment. Expect to be called 'gazelle' (probably based on the Arabic '*ghouzela*', meaning pretty) – the local equivalent of 'sweetheart'.

INDEX

INDEX